KINGDOM
RISING

BOOKS BY TODD BENTLEY

Kingdom Rising

Journey Into the Miraculous

Reality of the Supernatural World

AVAILABLE FROM DESTINY IMAGE PUBLISHERS

KINGDOM
RISING

MAKING THE KINGDOM
REAL IN YOUR LIFE

TODD BENTLEY

DESTINY IMAGE® PUBLISHERS, INC.
P.O. Box 310, Shippensburg, PA 17257-0310

"Speaking to the Purposes of God for this Generation and for the Generations to Come."

This book and all other Destiny Image, Revival Press, Mercy Place, Fresh Bread, Destiny Image Fiction, and Treasure House books are available at Christian bookstores and distributors worldwide.

For a U.S. bookstore nearest you, call 1-800-722-6774.

For more information on foreign distributors, call 717-532-3040.

Reach us on the Internet: www.destinyimage.com.

ISBN 10: 0-7684-2718-5

ISBN 13: 978-0-7684-2718-9

For Worldwide Distribution, Printed in the U.S.A.

1 2 3 4 5 6 7 8 9 10 11 / 12 11 10 09 08

DEDICATION

Be exalted, O God, above the heavens;
let Your glory be above all the earth (Psalm 57:11).

ACKNOWLEDGMENTS

Utmost thanks to my Abba Father for His perfect gifts to me and His perfect work in and through me. To the Holy Spirit for His sweet fellowship, for mentoring me in the ministry, and for teaching me all of the revelatory truths I've shared in this book.

Special thanks also to:

My beautiful wife, Shonnah, and my three wonderful children—Lauralee, Esther, and Elijah—for sharing me with the world.

My parents, Darcia and Dave Bentley. Mom, who endlessly champions me and *rushes* to help me fulfill the many visions God gives me. For her eye to detail, gift of creativity, her encouragement, and for looking after the publishing details of my books and writing. Dad who tirelessly accompanies me all over the world and without fail supports me in all of the work God has called me to.

The countless great men and women of faith of today who have encouraged, mentored, counseled, and inspired me, and who have interceded and prayed for me. People like Bob Jones, Bill Johnson, Patricia King, Heidi Baker, James Goll, Mahesh Chavda, Che Ahn, and many others who have shared their wisdom and counsel with me over the years.

My writer/editor, Shae Cooke, for her help in fulfilling God's vision for this teaching, for editing, articulating, and reworking my many words.

My Fresh Fire family—all those who work and serve so hard alongside me in this ministry in our offices and at crusades and conferences.

My ministry Partners—who through their faithful giving enable all of us to work together in this heavenly call of bringing down Heaven on earth in my generation for the glory of the Lord and the advancement of His Kingdom.

You, the reader, filled with an extraordinary obsession for God, who are willing to move into the limitless glory of living, moving, and having your being in the Kingdom of God. For allowing God to remove the boundaries so that He can expose you to the unbelievable supernatural realities of Kingdom living.

Don, Micki, Jonathan, Dean, and the entire Destiny Image team for your creativity, patience, vision, and relentless pursuit of excellence in all that you do for the kingdom purposes of God.

ENDORSEMENTS

I greatly enjoyed reading Todd's book. I don't encourage people to read it all at once because you would miss several really good points. Todd reveals that the Kingdom of God is not word but it is the Spirit Word. As Todd shares the word, the Holy Spirit establishes it because he has a gifting of faith. He faces many obstacles but overcomes them with the Word and the Spirit. This is a book that should really add faith to all who read it. Todd shows that he is just as common as all the rest of us are. But he believes in his faith and in this book he writes of all the signs and wonders that have taken place in his ministry. It's time the Body of Christ begins to believe and to do the things Todd is doing. It's time for power evangelism, and Todd has broken the trail for others to follow.

BOB JONES

Pastor

Todd Bentley's book on the Kingdom encourages us to all pursue the promise of God's Kingdom coming to earth as it is in Heaven now. What a joy it is to watch Todd call sons and daughters to their destinies in God! Todd has radically led the way through his own life. If you are hungry, this book will affect the way you live. It will propel you to seek greater intimacy with God and to desire Him above all else. Todd's new book provides rich and powerful fuel for all those wanting to move in the greater realms of Kingdom realities. While reading it I immediately sensed a longing to pursue an even deeper friendship with God.

HEIDI BAKER, PhD

Director, Iris Ministries

Contents

~

ENDNOTES

1. Chapter content originally published by Todd Bentley, "The War Anointing: Spiritual Victory Behind Enemy Lines." *Voice of the Prophetic*, December 2006. Copyright 2006 by Todd Bentley. Reprinted by permission of ElijahList Publications.

2. Chapter content originally published by Todd Bentley, "The Day of Manifestation—Impartation of Favor." *Voice of the Prophetic*, January 2007.

By many people's standards Todd Bentley is still a young man. Yet he is very seasoned in life and ministry. He has successfully contended in private for a Gospel of power which in turn has given him public victories that have benefited the Body of Christ at large. It would be fair to say that many who have labored in the same fields for a lifetime have not seen the measure of fruitfulness that has been given to Todd. Why? While Todd is known largely for the miracles that accompany his ministry, he is known in Heaven by his passion for the presence of God. His willingness to devote significant amounts of time to being saturated in God's glory has captured the Father's attention. As a result God has visited him over and over again with visions, trances, dreams, and other ecstatic experiences, all sowing into his call to invade the impossible. The bottom line is, Todd is a lover of God—he is God's friend.

Throughout history there have been many wonderful healing evangelists. They loved God and His Word, and they were used to bringing amazing miracles into people's lives. But most of them were not known for being good Bible teachers. It is worth noting that God has chosen Todd to be both a worker of miracles and a teacher of the Word. He carries significant biblical insight. This is what makes his writings so important to us, not the least of which is this book, *Kingdom Rising*. His writings contain revelation from Scripture, emphasizing what the Holy Spirit is emphasizing. Most importantly, his insights were not formed in a classroom as a theorist, but instead on his knees at the front lines of battle, where truth becomes proven and the Kingdom advances significantly.

This is that which brings salvation to a soul, demonstrates miracles with regularity, and brings transformation to entire cities. It is this message that is not satisfied with the number of bodies in church sanctuaries on Sunday morning, but is instead moved only by the impact of those believers on society.

Saying what the Father is saying is the model that Jesus set for us to follow. When we preach the right message, God shows up to reinforce it. The *Gospel of salvation* has been preached faithfully for centuries. But the message Jesus commissioned His disciples to preach was the *Gospel of the Kingdom.* While our conversion is the greatest of all miracles, salvation is included in the larger message of the Kingdom. It starts with, "Repent, for the Kingdom of Heaven is at hand." The salvation message tends to focus on going to Heaven, while the message of the *Kingdom* is about bringing Heaven to earth. This is our commission, as found in the prayer model Jesus gave His disciples in Matthew 6:10, "on earth as it is in Heaven." Heaven is my destiny, but bringing Heaven is my assignment.

This message is the most essential message of the hour. In a world filled with chaos and conflict, people need to know that Jesus has already won a victory over every enemy of humankind. He is the King of kings and the Lord of lords over all that exists...right now. His victories were obtained for our benefit.

Kingdom Rising is a book that helps to address this huge need in the Body of Christ. Todd gives us profound instruction, testimonies that show "how to," and the inspiration needed to pursue with endurance. The reader is sure to explode with hunger for more, realizing that God's intention for each of us is greater than we've ever imagined. In *Kingdom Rising*, Todd's unique insights into the ways of the Holy Spirit qualify him to bring us these truths. I am excited to see this book hit the bookstores, as it will make a major contribution in helping us transition from the mere doctrine of "being seated in heavenly places in Christ" into an ongoing experience that equips and empowers.

BILL JOHNSON
Senior Pastor
Bethel Church, Redding, California
Author, *When Heaven Invades Earth,*
The Supernatural Power of a Transformed Mind,
Dreaming With God, Strengthen Yourself in the Lord,
and *Face to Face with God*

Part I

THE DECLARATION OF THE KINGDOM OF GOD

I N T R O D U C T I O N

ENTER THE KINGDOM ZONE
MATTHEW 5-7

We cannot unleash our awesome potential and rise to our supernatural Kingdom callings without the foundation of Kingdom knowledge that Christ gave us in His Sermon on the Mount, starting with the Beatitudes. Before delving further into study, I encourage you to read chapters five through seven in the Book of Matthew in the New Testament, where you'll find that Christ gave us a set of supernatural standards to live by.

The Beatitudes are like the foreword to Christ's Sermon on the Mount. This Sermon some refer to as the Constitution, Charter, or Declaration of the Kingdom of God, and it defines what should be the character of the sons and daughters of the King with as many as 21 principles for Kingdom living. The message in the Beatitudes (the opening sentences of the Sermon on the Mount) describes the quality of life possible for every supernatural Kingdom dweller, and it's obvious that it requires a radical shift or change of nature—Christ's nature being worked in and through us—inwardly and outwardly. It's about a transformational shift of the sons and daughters of God from the kingdom of darkness into the Kingdom of light. It's about shedding all worldly ambition and radically and obsessively pursuing God and His plans and purposes.

When we seek first His Kingdom and righteousness, all other things are added to us as well (see Matt. 6:33). Each of the blessings listed in the *Beatitudes* (a Latin word meaning "happy, blessed") are for every believer to apply and develop. Christ talks about sin in speaking about the poor in spirit. He speaks about repentance in "they that mourn." The meek He describes as not weak but strong in the surrender to God for salvation. He encourages us to hunger and thirst after righteousness, which simply means to yearn to become more like Christ! We are called to be merciful ones, always forgiving of others. We are to be pure in heart, striving daily to live the holy life, separated unto God. Kingdom citizens are to be peacemakers and faithful under stress. Those who change and who develop the Kingdom mindset will live in the promised blessings of God. Blessed are you if you strive for these things!

SHIFT OF THOUGHT

Consider how He encourages us to change our thought processes! It's cut and dried and drives home the message that if we pursue Him with all of our heart, our worries are "out the door, man!" He tells us to seek first the Kingdom of God and His righteousness, and we essentially will never have to worry about another thing in our entire lives. He tells us not to worry about our life anymore because *life is* the Kingdom of God and His righteousness.

As faithful citizens in His Kingdom, we don't have to worry about provision, about what we will eat or drink, about having enough clothing, or about our body, because He says that life is much more than those things (see Matt. 6:25). Now that's a radical shift right there, especially in this inflationary day and age. It's hard not to worry about these things because jobs come and go, the economy seesaws, and even many two-income families just can't get ahead financially. But Jesus says that we don't have to worry about those things anymore! He tells us to look at the birds of the air and how the Father feeds them, and He says, are we not of more value than they are? (See Matthew 6:26.) He tells us to consider how splendidly He clothes the lilies of the fields and how much more He is able to do for us (see Matt. 6:28-30). Why worry when we have the Creator of the Universe caring for us as His children and anticipating our needs? How much more important are we to Him than the creatures of the earth that He already takes such good care of? He knows our needs, and He knows how to care for them. The Kingdom of God is such that there's never a need to worry about tomorrow while in His care. To know God is to know no worry!

Jesus gave us a model prayer first to help us to recognize to whom we pray: God, our Father in Heaven! What a revelation this must have been to the people of the day. Imagine accessing God as a Father without any earthly go-between!

> *Our Father in heaven, hallowed be Your name. Your kingdom come. Your will be done on earth as it is in heaven. Give us this day our daily bread. And forgive us our debts, as we forgive our debtors. And do not lead*

us into temptation, but deliver us from the evil one. For Yours is the kingdom and the power and the glory forever. Amen (Matthew 6:9-13).

It's a privilege to call Him our Father! It's a privilege and a divine advantage to be a child of the King, a son or daughter of the God Most High! He's given us access to Himself through Jesus and access to the blessings of Heaven and the reality of the supernatural realms of God.

In the early days, it was unusual for the Jewish people to call God "Father" because it was too intimate, but in that model prayer, Jesus is demonstrating that it's OK to call God your Father—He desires intimacy with you! He wants you to know who you are in Him! When you pray, pray as His child: "My Father in Heaven…."

When we say, "Our Father *in Heaven*," it reminds us of His holiness and His glory; so He is indeed our Father, but even more importantly, our *glorious and heavenly* Father.

Pray With Passion!

We're to pray with a passion for the Father's glory and His plans and purposes! Hallowed be Your name! Your Kingdom come! Always His name, His Kingdom, and His will should have top priority in our prayers and come first before we come to Him with our needs. We must lift Him up higher than any other name, including our own! We must be of the Kingdom mindset, thinking about His plans and Kingdom purposes. Of course "Your Kingdom come, your will be done on earth as it is in Heaven," the underlying theme of *Kingdom Rising,* is about the invasive and increasing nature of the Kingdom of God displayed on earth—His will, rule, and eternal reign. For His is the Kingdom and the power and the glory forever! We are to praise God and give credit to Him and His name only, the Kingdom and the power and the glory!

Christ also shows us by this prayer that we can come to the Father with our needs for provision, for forgiveness, and for His strength and might when temptation comes. But He assures us that, in the face of temptation, we will never have more than we can bear and He is always near.

SONSHIP

The underlying thread woven into the fine tapestry of Christ's words is a shift and change of mindset and character that is His life being worked in and through us as we seek the Kingdom of God and His righteousness first, because then all of the things He lists will be added unto us.

In the unleashing of our supernatural potential, it's vital that we learn to discern what is constructive to our spiritual character and to the will of God in the earth. It's not a question of what is right or wrong or a set of rules and laws that we have to live by. Rather, it is about conforming in character and aligning ourselves to Kingdom principles that advance the Kingdom of God in the hearts of people. Our aim should always be first to love the Lord and lift high the name of the Lord throughout the earth, glorifying Him in all that we do—and then to love one another.

When Kingdom ways are in our step, God blesses us. It's the principle of sowing and reaping, and what we sow, we'll reap (see 2 Cor. 9:6; Gal. 6:7-8). We are no longer under the law, and thus we are blessed if we do the Father's will and not blessed if we don't! "Blessed are they that…" (see Matt. 5:1-11). Cut and dry! What we sow to the flesh, we reap, and so on.

It's essential therefore that you're grounded and well-versed in the Kingdom principles, for they lay a good foundation for what I'm about to expound on and teach you. Only if you understand and live within these Kingdom principles will you experience breakthrough and empowerment and the full release of your supernatural divine potential to transform the earth for the glory of the Lord. Following and fulfilling Kingdom principles sets you up for amazing Kingdom blessings and benefits, not only in the natural, but also in the supernatural things of God!

You have help! The Holy Spirit is with you to guide, encourage, lead, and help you live by these principles. They will set you free! They will grow with you and go with you as blueprints and strategies for invading the earth with the glory of the Lord! They will launch you into an awesome destiny as a Kingdom citizen in a Kingdom nation, God's nation!

ONLY ONE STANDARD

There is only one standard by which we are to live: God's Kingdom standard. That divine standard calls us to accept radical change in the way we think, live, and breathe. We must transform our mindsets from that of the natural realm to the supernatural realm of

God, which is the reality of the Kingdom, for this is the only way that we can fulfill our calling and purpose, which ultimately is to follow Jesus. I hope that this book opens your eyes, lifts the veil, increases your understanding, and excites you into living in the reality of one who is a citizen in the Kingdom nation of God and a joint heir with Christ of all of its blessings.

"By faith," Abraham, when God called him, obeyed by going out to a place that he was to receive for an inheritance, and he wasn't even quite sure where that place was! By faith, the Bible tells us that he lived as an alien in the land of promise—and you're no different. You and I are aliens in the world, but not for long because the land of promise is advancing, accelerating, taking ground, and filling the earth. Yes, we're dwelling in tents with fellow heirs of the very same promise, but our goal and our hearts should be bent on searching and looking for the city which has foundations, whose architect and builder is God! (See Hebrews 11:8-10.)

I pray that the Holy Spirit speaks to your heart and that the prophetic revelatory teachings I'm about to share with you will catapult you into realms of Kingdom realities that will unleash you into your supernatural Kingdom calling for the transformation of the world around you.

In this, the first of two *Kingdom Rising* books, it is my heart that the foundations we lay will inspire you enough to thrust you into the dynamics of living a supernatural, overcoming, triumphant, victorious, peculiar, and spectacular life as you were created to live it, having the mind of Christ and ready to step into the very way God thinks.

The sequel to *Kingdom Rising,* which will be published in the spring/summer of 2009, will fire you up in greater ways for harvest and evangelism. We'll explore in detail the supernatural aspects of the Kingdom of God available to you, with keys for developing a supernatural lifestyle and a greater sensitivity to the Spirit of God. We'll battle for the mind, heart, and emotions, and use our authority strategically in the battle and come out as conquerors winning the prize of great value—possessing the mind of Christ. You'll appreciate why having His mind is essential to living a supernatural lifestyle daily—why having 20/20 spiritual vision is vital as you participate in what could be the greatest global harvest this earth has ever seen.

My prayer is that *Kingdom Rising* and its sequel will cause a rise to action in your heart, as you arise and influence the world for the Kingdom of Heaven. God is assembling His sons and daughters to advance the Kingdom forcefully. New revelations of His love are coming to you that will bring Kingdom vision and divine strategy that will bring glory to the Father and God's Kingdom to earth.

Enter the Kingdom zone, and rise to that higher realm and purpose that God has called you to!

THE REALITY OF THE KINGDOM

Have you ever wanted to taste Heaven? I mean, really experience it? Do you dream about it, about what it's like? Do you long to see Jesus, the throne, the streets paved with gold, the great cloud of witnesses, the sea of glass like crystal, the mansions, the glory, the splendor, and the majesty of God? Do you think about that joyful place where there is no sickness, no disease, no poverty, where you can live victoriously without worry?

You're not alone in your dreams and hopes for eternity. Most of us long for that day when we enter into Heaven. We're almost of a rapture mindset, and for the most part we live day-to-day in a survival mode, hanging on until that glorious day when Jesus catches us up into the clouds and out of this big old mess. We envision how we will live a victorious life, a truly overcoming one. Who doesn't look forward to that day? I know that I can't wait until I get to that place in Heaven, whether Jesus catches me up in the Rapture, or if I die before He comes.

Yes, as a born again and steadfast believer in Christ Jesus, you will see and experience those things. But why wait? Why live life only with a Heaven-in-the-future mindset? You can experience Heaven now. Your born-again experience was an invitation to see and experience the Kingdom of God now, on earth. We've limited the born-again experience to "one day I have an inheritance in Heaven." However, when we're born again, we enter the Kingdom of God and experience it in the here and now.

We can't see anything about God's Kingdom until we're born again. Jesus told a Pharisee named Nicodemus, "I assure you, most solemnly I tell you, that unless a person is born again (anew, from above), he cannot ever see (know, be acquainted with, and experience) the Kingdom of God" (John 3:3 AMP). This new spiritual birth and the ability to see the Kingdom of God go hand in hand.

Jesus went on to say to Nicodemus in verse 5: "Most assuredly, I say to you, unless one is born of water and the Spirit, he cannot enter the Kingdom of God" (John 3:5).

It's about now, just as much as it is about the future heavenly residence. The resurrection of Jesus brought you into the fullness of the Kingdom so that you don't have to just dream about meeting Jesus or experiencing Kingdom life. You can experience Him and live it right here, right now, on earth. You don't have to wait until you die or are raptured to receive your heavenly inheritance.

I want to challenge your mindset concerning the way you might be thinking, maybe most of the time, about the Kingdom of God. Did you know that your thoughts and the information that you believe to be true forge your mindset? So what is your *Kingdom mindset*? Present, future, or both?

Our Heaven-in-the-future mindset limits us, because in reality, all of its power is available to us today. We tend to think as the

Pharisees did when they asked Jesus when the Kingdom of God would come. He answered them and said, "The Kingdom of God does not come with observation; nor will they say, 'See here!' or 'See there!'" (Luke 17:20-21a).

HEAVEN ON EARTH

Jesus prayed, "Your Kingdom come. Your will be done on earth as it is in heaven" (Matt. 6:10). The Kingdom of God is Heaven on earth. Think about that—in Heaven on earth. We have to learn how to synchronize Heaven and earth; it's what the born-again experience is—living in the reality of Heaven now, on the earth, and not just "ultimately I will enter the Kingdom of God."

It's a present reality just as much as it is a future one. You can see, feel, touch, taste, hear, and experience the Kingdom. Jesus Christ, the King of kings and the King of glory, experienced it, and so can we. In fact, His Kingdom comes to *invade* your world, and you are commanded to forcefully take ground for the Kingdom. The message of the hour is the King and His Kingdom! The Kingdom of God is reality "as it is [already functioning] in Heaven" displayed on earth. "Your kingdom come. Your will be done on earth as it is in Heaven" (Matt. 6:10).

ETERNAL RULE AND REIGN OF GOD

The Kingdom of God[1] is the reign and rule of God, and it existed before the beginning of time. His Kingdom is eternal and unchanging, just as God Himself is eternal and unchanging. (See Jeremiah 10:10; Daniel 4:34.) The Kingdom of God has existed from all eternity (see Ps. 74:12), and He has prepared His Kingdom for us since the creation of the world (see Matt. 25:34). The Kingdom is the reality of the never-ending, unshakeable, and unchanging God of the Universe. It is the reality of the call from a life outside of His nature and person to one reconnected into that Kingdom existence that never ended. Although sin affected the manifestation of the Kingdom on earth, the Kingdom in Heaven didn't change. God's will always was, is, and always will be done in Heaven, but His complete will being done on earth was compromised in Adam's sin.

Not only is it a Kingdom that existed; it still exists! It is a present Kingdom that lasts throughout the generations, and from generation to generation where God is enthroned eternally as King: "The Lord sat enthroned at the Flood, and the Lord sits as King forever" (Ps. 29:10). It is the rule of God—the age to come—and His Kingdom invades the world's kingdom, called the devil's "present evil age" (see Gal. 1:4), thanks to the death and resurrection of Christ Jesus—the Son of God who came to redeem humankind and bring the Kingdom of God into the earth. The Kingdom operates today in Heaven, of course, but it also operates on earth now through believers, and it will have a final consummation and perfection at the end when Christ will have delivered up the Kingdom to God. (See 1 Corinthians 15:24.)

The Kingdom of God and the Kingdom of Heaven often signify the same thing but are sometimes used in different contexts or senses. The Kingdom of Heaven is a part of the Kingdom of God. It transcends much more than a "celestial place" out there in the heavens and encompasses much more than we usually realize.

You're already familiar with the future Heaven, but these references also denote the spiritual rule that the Messiah came down to establish in the world—that Gospel Kingdom of salvation that would advance and prevail over all the nations of the earth. Hence, there are certain places on earth where His Kingdom and Presence manifest to a high degree (which I will examine in a later chapter).

While it has eschatological application as far as God's rule at all levels in Heaven and on earth, the Kingdom also applies to us as God's rule and reign in our individual hearts. Just as Jesus answered the Pharisees, He's telling you "Don't wait to enter the Kingdom, because it is in you. The Kingdom of Heaven is at hand" (see Matt. 3:2).

The Kingdom of Heaven is within us *now*.

You, as a born-again believer, are a Kingdom citizen—but are you a Kingdom ambassador, and do you live as a citizen of the Kingdom of Heaven? Do you live, breathe, walk, talk, act, and represent God as His ambassador in everything you do or say? When God first expanded His Kingdom by creating the earth, Adam was the first Kingdom ambassador. We know that Adam walked with God in the Garden, and God gave him dominion (power, authority, control, and so on) over the earth. Do you demonstrate Kingdom power? What about authority? Have you tapped into the inheritance, the blessings that are yours?

For Lack of Knowledge

Few people do—not for lack of desire, but lack of knowledge. God wants you to hunger to know more and to experience the same power and boldness that Jesus had to heal, to deliver, to preach, to teach, and to overcome, because He wants you to fill as much of the earth with as much of the Kingdom as you can. You are His beloved child and as such should be willing and ready to push as far as you can until the Lord says, "No more!" (See Matthew 11:12.)

The Kingdom is here, now. Get out there and go for it! As Jesus was His Son, you are His son or daughter, and you have inherited the same keys to the Kingdom.

God is the King *of* Heaven and all creation. Jesus is the king *from* Heaven on earth and heir to all of the kingdoms of Heaven and to all of creation! We, the redeemed sons and daughters, are the subjects of Christ's Kingdom. All that is upon the earth is the domain God gave to us to rule and reign with Him. As mature, redeemed Kingdom subjects, we are rulers, ruling as kings under the King of kings and Lord of lords.

We can't work our way up to kingship; we have to be born into it, and we have to grow up in it to fulfill our destiny of ruling and reigning with Him.

Heaven is the order of things eternal. It is a realm of the impossible and the everlasting. We live under its protective canopy and the rule and reign of God in our hearts and lives. Its banner is love and it's growing, advancing, moving, and seeking to fill every part of your life.

Hunger and Advance

Are you yearning for something greater than yourself? Are you desperate for your life to have spiritual power and eternal significance? Do you want to rise above the ordinary and the temporal? Are you constantly dissatisfied? Great! You're hungry for Jesus and the Kingdom of God, even though you may not know it! It's because, as a Spirit-filled believer in Christ, you are a Kingdom person, and you won't be satisfied until you are drawn to Kingdom principles and Kingdom pursuits. Are you hearing what the Lord has to say about the Kingdom of God? He welcomes and invites you to learn more and live it now. The key is to hunger and advance!

I hungered. I spent hours, days, and months yearning for His presence. I soaked, waited, sat at His feet, cried out to Him, and asked to see Him, to know Him, to touch Him, and for Him to touch me. He did! The glory liquid honey cloud of His presence overwhelmed me at times. I pursued Him with everything I had, with all of my might. I wouldn't leave Him alone, just as the crowds wouldn't leave Jesus alone. They hungered to hear more about the Kingdom of God. Even when He retreated to quiet places they sought Him out, desperate in their desire to know more about what He had and what He knew: "But when the multitudes knew *it*, they followed Him; and He received them and spoke to them about the Kingdom of God, and healed those who had need of healing" (Luke 9:11).

Jesus not only spoke of the Kingdom, but also demonstrated kingdom power. Notice the "and" part of the verse: "*and* healed those who had *need of* healing."

He welcomed them and healed them, and the revelation of their newfound knowledge changed them and changed the world. My revelation and my newfound knowledge transformed me. I'm living proof as an ex-drug addict and tough biker-type dude turned determined biker-dude-evangelist and revivalist bent on seeing God's glory invade lives! When I gave my life to Jesus in my drug dealer's trailer at age 18, God immediately set me free of addiction to drugs and alcohol. I didn't have one craving or one pang of withdrawal; I mean, I was saved, man!

Immediately, I dove into the Word. Just coming off the street as a drug addict, I didn't know anything about Church history or revival, the anointing to heal, or the presence of God, but I hungered to know more about Jesus. Then, I received the baptism of the Holy Spirit at a Full Gospel Business Men's meeting, and my hunger grew even more. Someone gave me Benny Hinn's book, *Good Morning Holy Spirit,* and revelation hit—I wanted to know more about this person of the Holy Spirit!

Benny's book piqued my curiosity, and I started to read every book I could get my hands on. Through Hinn's ministry, I learned about Kathryn Khulman. I read books by Oral Roberts and Kenneth Hagin, and I learned about other giants of faith, past and present, who had affected revival—who had healing and evangelistic ministries.

Reading about Evangelist Reinhard Bonnke blew me away! Even today, he reaches millions in single crusades alone, seeing hundreds of thousands of people healed, saved, and delivered. What astonished and moved me the most, though, was the involvement of the presence of God in his meetings. "Lord, that's what I want…" I cried out to God. I wanted God's presence to move through stadiums, in the marketplaces—for hundreds of thousands of people to hunger and thirst after, to experience, and to know His presence! This has been my heart since I started in ministry.

Here I was an unlearned, uneducated teen who'd discovered the key that wrought such authority from Christ to heal, to advance the Kingdom of God. All of these giants of faith had been with Jesus. This revelation burned in my heart, and I just wanted to be with Him! I held on, asked God for a ministry of His presence, and invited the Holy Spirit to fill my life so that I could become one that would carry His presence throughout the world.

I'd cry out to God, "I'll pay the price—I'll pay the price Lord! I'll pay the price for the anointing!" Yes, I was ready and willing to pay any price for the anointing to take the Kingdom by force. Man, I was hungry for that ministry of His presence, and I was a willing student. I learned to move in my healing anointing by developing a personal intimate fellowship with the Holy Spirit—I didn't want to take a single breath without the Holy Spirit! As I grew in relationship with the Holy Spirit, asking Him questions and coming to know Him as a person, everything began to flow like a river—everything fell effortlessly into place for my ministry.

Today, I'm preaching in stadiums! We're in the midst of revival in Lakeland, Florida, where we're seeing tens of thousands come for the presence of God. Every day we're seeing the advancement of the Kingdom of God with every teaching, with every testimony, with every Word of God we're sending forth, and these things are transforming multitudes.

THE KINGDOM: ACTIVE TODAY

In the parable of the mustard seed, Jesus explained that the Kingdom, like the mustard seed, starts small and grows quietly, hidden like yeast (see Mark 4:30-32; 26-29; Matt. 13:33). These parables Jesus spoke suggest that the Kingdom of Heaven is a reality before it comes in a powerful and awesome way. So, not only is it a future reality, but it has reality here and now.

Jesus demonstrated this reality when He said, after casting out demons, "If I cast out demons by the Spirit of God, surely the Kingdom of God has come upon you" (Matt. 12:28). In other words, He was telling us that the Kingdom is here, and the proof was in the casting out of the demons.

Do you remember what Jesus said after John was put into prison, as Jesus arrived in Galilee to preach the Gospel of the Kingdom of God? He said, "The time is fulfilled, and the Kingdom of God is at hand. Repent, and believe in the Gospel" (Mark 1:15).

Proof of the Kingdom now is still evident in the Body of Christ today. This is exciting—if we cast out demons by the Spirit of God, then the Kingdom of God *is*—present tense—working here, now. The Kingdom of God, by the power of God's Spirit, is still at work today in its authoritative power over the enemy's kingdom.

We also scripturally see that it's an active Kingdom, because Jesus said that the good news of the Kingdom of God *is being* preached and everyone *is forcing* their way into it (see Luke 16:16 NIV). The King James Version describes it as everyone *pressing* into it. In Matthew 11:12, Jesus uses the present tense to say, "From the days of John the Baptist until *now* the kingdom of heaven *suffers* violence and the violent *take* it by force."

The Kingdom is a present-day reality just as real as it was in Jesus' day.

It's Our Inheritance

We are created in His image as spirit beings, and creation recognizes us as children of God. Consider that when Adam and Eve walked in the Garden before the Fall, creation bowed to them for they were God's own.

As believers, we are the Church, the called out ones, those delivered from the consequences of destruction brought on by Adam. The Church isn't comprised of four walls and a steeple, but of people brought out of an existence void of God's nature and person and into the very divine nature of God. Anything contrary to that is a destructive opposing force and outside of the Kingdom realm.

As His children, we are not here on earth to eke out a life or to scrape and survive and make it to Heaven. We're here to rule, reign, and prosper because God created this world for us. We are not orphans, nor should we have an orphan mindset of being desolate or lost, of fearing or losing, of being sick or bound. We are children of the King, created in His very image, born of and filled with His very Spirit. We have authority on earth, and are not weak beings at the mercy of the world, because we are not of it. We are of the Kingdom nation that extends far beyond the earth and its principalities and heavens. Jesus said Himself that we are in this world but are not *of this world,* that we are from a totally other dimension in the Spirit (see John 17:14; 18:36).

In fact, we are *sons and daughters of God,* led by the Spirit of God and *subject to* the law of the Holy Spirit in Christ Jesus. In Paul's letter to the Romans, he repeatedly mentions the "sons of God," and even tells us who they are:

For as many are led by the Spirit of God, these are sons of God. For you did not receive the spirit of bondage again to fear, but you received the Spirit of adoption by whom we cry out, "Abba, Father." The Spirit Himself bears witness with our spirit that we are children of God (Romans 8:14-16).

The Holy Spirit empowers us to live according to "the law of the Spirit of life in Christ Jesus." If we walk in the power of the Spirit, we fulfill the requirements of the law.

For the law of the Spirit of life in Christ Jesus has made me free from the law of sin and death. For what the law could not do in that it was weak through the flesh, God did by sending His own Son in the likeness of sinful flesh, on account of sin: He condemned sin in the flesh, that the righteous requirement of the law might be fulfilled in us who do not walk according to the flesh but according to the Spirit (Romans 8:2-4).

Because Jesus lives, you can live according to "the law of the Spirit of life." The resurrection life of Jesus brings us into the *fullness of the Kingdom of God.* It imparted to us—by the Holy Spirit—life to overcome all that comes against us.

A Spiritual Kingdom

The nature of the Kingdom of God is spiritual. We see Jesus

speaking of the spiritual aspect in the account of Nicodemus, where Jesus taught him about how to enter the Kingdom God.

Nicodemus, a Pharisee and ruler of the Jews, came to Jesus one night and asked Jesus, "Rabbi, we know that You are a teacher come from God; for no one can do these signs that You do unless God is with him" (John 3:2). Jesus told him that "unless one is born again, he cannot see the kingdom of God" (John 3:3). However, Nicodemus, still not quite understanding, asked, "How can a man be born when he is old? Can he enter a second time into his mother's womb and be born?" (John 3:4). Jesus explained and said that "unless one is born of water and the Spirit, he cannot enter the kingdom of God" (John 3:5).

We are born of the Spirit, thus we are spirit as God is Spirit. We are spirits having a human experience, not humans having a spiritual one. In the following breath, Jesus said, "That which is born of the flesh is flesh, and that which is born of the Spirit is spirit" (John 3:6). Jesus is making a very important statement here. You are spirit! You are not a human being with a spirit trying to strengthen your spirit, because what is born of the Spirit *is* spirit. Your first nature as a believer is that of spirit. You are spirit. Think on that. As spirit, the restrictions of a natural body shouldn't limit you. We must change our way of thinking to grasp these Kingdom principles.

God intended all along for us to see through the eyes of the Kingdom of Heaven, through an eternal perception rather than a limited earthly one. By our earthly perception, if we were told we had an incurable disease, it would be the end for us. With a heavenly or Kingdom perception, we know that God's power can heal—today, now, here on earth—without having to wait for our perfect bodies in Heaven.

As a Christian, you are a citizen of Heaven and not subject to the laws and limitations of the world in which you dwell. God has made you a citizen and representative of His government and His world. Though you live in your body, you're not from here...you are Kingdom born.

KINGDOM PERSPECTIVES

"The kingdom of God is at hand" (Mark 1:15). "At hand" means "always near or nearby." It is close because the presence and personality of the Holy Spirit manifest the Kingdom—the creative power of Heaven on earth.

The Kingdom Jesus talked about was not of this world. To Pilate, Jesus answered, "My kingdom is not of this world. If My kingdom were of this world, My servants would fight, so that I should not be delivered to the Jews; but now My kingdom is not from here" (John 18:36).

In other words, Jesus was saying that the things that went on around Him, those things that were of the earthly kingdom, did not influence Him. The Bible also says that we have been conveyed (or "translated" in the KJV) from the kingdom of darkness into the Kingdom of light (see Col. 1:13). We use the word *translated* when we think about converting words from one language to another. We're converted from one world to another. He has rescued us from the kingdom of darkness and brought us into the Kingdom of light. In this new Kingdom, people speak an entirely different language that bears no relation to the language that we used to speak before; that's why we have to press in for the renewing of our mindset. We must begin to see things from a different and supernatural perspective, from the vantage point of sitting in heavenly places with Christ (see Eph. 2:6).

The Jews were familiar with the Kingdom of God, but Jesus gave it new meaning when describing it to Nicodemus. He said that God's Kingdom was invisible to most people and that to experience it, or even to understand it, a person had to be renewed by God's Spirit (see John 3:3). Even though the Kingdom of God is a spiritual realm, because we are spirit, we can learn how to touch, access, and experience that invisible realm daily. God wants to answer us when we call on Him. Because we are communicating spirit to Spirit, He answers us and shows us things we could never see, feel, touch, or hear with our natural senses. He says, "Call to Me, and I will answer you, and show you great and mighty things, which you do not know" (Jer. 33:3).

Wow!

God commands us to set our minds on those things which are above, where Christ is. Where is Christ? In heavenly places:

> *If then you were raised with Christ, seek those things which are above, where Christ is, sitting at the right hand of God. Set your mind on things above, not on things on the earth. For you died, and your life is hidden with Christ in God. When Christ Who is our life appears, than you also will appear with Him in glory* (Colossians 3:1-4).

43

If we set our minds on something, it's usually because it's something we desire or seek. Things that we seek, we usually focus on. God wants us to focus on the things above, not on the things of this earth. We are to seek heavenly places and the things of Heaven. It's a biblical invitation, a command, to seek the supernatural things of God, of the Kingdom of Heaven. If we focus instead on earth, on the things of this world, we can't enter into the things of the Spirit.

We will rise above our natural circumstances and live in greater victory as we respond to God's invitation to come higher in spirit, to seek to hear from Heaven, and to receive spiritual revelation and experiences.

Revelation is unfolding moment-by-moment concerning Jesus Christ, the King of kings and the King of Glory, and His Kingdom. The Kingdom of God is the will of God being done on the earth. Jesus said, "He who has seen Me has seen the Father" (John 14:9). He went about doing good and healing those oppressed by the devil because that was the Kingdom of God (see Acts 10:38). Healing sickness and disease was the Father's will. Healing *every* sickness and disease is the Kingdom of God. If you cast out devils by the Spirit of God, the Kingdom of God has come upon you.

WELCOMING THE KINGDOM

Jesus accomplished the will of the Father and only did what He saw His Father doing (see John 5:19). He modeled the vision of what He saw in Heaven, and He brought the Kingdom of God to earth. When He taught His disciples how to pray, He gave them an important key to releasing the Kingdom of God in the earth. He said, "In this manner, therefore, pray: Our Father in heaven, hallowed be Your name. Your kingdom come. Your will be done on earth as it is in heaven" (Matt. 6:9-10). He didn't just say, "Father, let Your Kingdom come." Jesus first honored the Father, and He prayed those words out of worship and intimacy. That's the key. He welcomed God's Kingdom to come because He knew that—for God's will to be done on earth as it is in Heaven—His Kingdom needed to be welcomed with a heart of worship and then invited to come.

The Kingdom of God is not in the earth right now *as it is* in Heaven, but we should want it to be and press in to advance it. When Jesus said we are to pray "Your Kingdom come," He was saying that it's not on the earth right now as it is in Heaven. In saying, "Your will be done," He was in effect saying, "It is My will that it would be on the earth now as it is in Heaven." So it is important for the Body of Christ to honor the Father just as Jesus did and then invite and welcome His Kingdom to come. "God, I welcome Your Kingdom. Please come into my world so that the earth begins to take on the image and the atmosphere of Heaven. Please let it be on earth for me now as it is in Heaven."

It is good and right to invite and welcome the rule of God to come as it is in Heaven, but we always must remember that the Kingdom of God comes when we walk in the center of God's will. The Kingdom of God can't come in power or in its fullness until we can truly say, "Your will be done, I surrender all." Until there is surrender and death to self, we'll never experience significant measures of "Your Kingdom come" in our lives.

What creates the atmosphere for relationship that brings the

Kingdom to earth? Praise and worship. Surrender and obedience. The Lord is on the throne in Heaven, and the earth is His footstool (see Isa. 66:1). We, the Body of Christ, connect the throne and the footstool so that the kingdoms of this world become the kingdoms of our Lord (see Rev. 11:15). We are the ones who establish the Kingdom, the dominion and authority of God on earth, by our actions, which will re-align those things already in Heaven with earth.

LIVING HEAVEN ON EARTH

Living in Heaven on earth should be a goal of every saint. We can ascend into this spiritual realm because we're invited to. Consider Jacob's dream at Bethel where he saw the ladder that reached to Heaven with the angels upon it ascending and descending (see Gen. 28:10-22). This was a prophetic picture of Heaven opening, made possible by Christ. This "Jacob's Ladder" anointing for believers is for today too, as we see in the Book of John: "And He said to him, 'Most assuredly, I say to you, hereafter you shall see Heaven open, and the angels of God ascending and descending upon the Son of Man'" (John 1:51). Jesus made that extraordinary statement while He was *on the earth*. Jesus was literally in Heaven on earth—that's how connected He was to God's invisible Kingdom.

Christ is that ladder, the way from earth to Heaven, the way Heaven sends messages to the world, and the way we must go to reach Heaven. Jesus made the way for us between earth and Heaven.[2] He said, "No one has ascended into Heaven, but He who descended from Heaven: the Son of Man" (John 3:13 NASB).

The ladder in Jacob's dream went from earth to Heaven. No one has ascended into Heaven except the Son of Man who has come down out of the heavens and who is *in* Heaven. It was in Heaven on earth. This is what the born-again experience is. In Heaven on earth. On earth as it is in Heaven! Living in the reality of Heaven now on earth is entering the Kingdom of God. He made the way for a clear and abundant revelation of God's will: that Heaven itself should be laid open and its mysteries, previously hidden in it from eternity, now be fully revealed. Through Christ, who was God manifested in the flesh, the lines of communication between Heaven and earth, the throne and the footstool, were established. Because of the Savior's resurrection, Heaven opened *to* earth, and Heaven opened *on* earth. This was the plea of Isaiah: "Oh, that You would rend the heavens! That You would come down! That the mountains might shake at Your presence" (Isa. 64:1).

We see the heavens descending after John baptized Jesus, too. What descended was a Kingdom of power, the power of God and of miracles, signs, wonders, dominion, and authority. This opening of Heaven and its coming to earth was later illustrated just before the death of Stephen at the hands of the Sanhedrin. He saw the glory of God because the heavens opened. He said, "Look! I see the heavens opened and the Son of Man standing at the right hand of God" (Acts 7:56). For him to see into the third heaven, he'd have to see with supernatural eyes, as Isaiah and Ezekiel saw. It could also be that Heaven came down to him, similar to when John saw the holy city, New Jerusalem "coming down out of Heaven from God..." (Rev. 21:2).

ACCESSING THE BLESSINGS IN HEAVENLY PLACES

The point is that God's door never closes. Heaven has issued an open invitation to come boldly before the throne to see and ascend into that invisible spiritual realm of the Kingdom of God (see Heb. 4:16). We're also invited to come as often as we want, because Christ's blood has given us free entrance. We have unrestricted access as often as we want. Under the Law, there were restrictions, but under the New Covenant, the priest no longer needs to enter the Most Holy Place once a year. We are all spiritual priests who can freely enter and lay hold of the many blessings found there.

Do you know how to access "every spiritual blessing in the heavenly places in Christ" that the Bible claims we have? (See Ephesians 1:3.) Many of us know that these blessings are there, but we don't believe deep down that they are for us. Nevertheless, God wants us to experience the fullness of these promises, and they should be reality to us. We lay hold of them by being with Christ Jesus in heavenly places. We can't lay hold of the inheritance of Heaven from the physical realm here on earth. It's only when we're experiencing the realm of Heaven, the Kingdom of God, that we can access its supernatural blessings and inheritance. The realm of Heaven has tremendous riches stored up, and God wants to open that supernatural resource "center" for us.

Are you ready and waiting for the Kingdom of God to invade your life? If it can happen to others, it can happen to you. The Kingdom of Heaven is at hand, it's near, and it's just a matter of breaking through the membrane between earth and Heaven.

CARRIERS OF THE KINGDOM

The natural mind, the carnal mind, the limitations of our flesh, distractions, and the world keep us from manifesting the fullness of God. Right now, you carry the Kingdom. It's not the future Kingdom, but the Kingdom of Heaven at hand—the Kingdom of God within you. The Holy Spirit wants you to receive a Kingdom mindset. The Kingdom springs up from within. The same Spirit that raised Jesus from the dead lives in you, and He quickens and brings life to your mortal flesh (see Rom. 8:11).

My life really changed when I began to meditate on this verse. I would take hours at a time just to focus on this one truth: the *same* Spirit. *The same Spirit* that anointed Jesus of Nazareth, *the same Spirit* that raised Jesus from the dead, lives in me. That means that right now I am carrying the Kingdom. I'm dangerous! You are dangerous!

LIVE IN CHRIST, DIE TO SELF, EXPERIENCE RESURRECTION

It's rather ironic, but soon after the new birth, a death experience comes along—death to self, death to our carnal nature, that "old man." But we can thank God for that resurrection that follows. Before I was baptized in water, someone told me that after I went under, I'd arise a new man. It was true. The convergence of those two acts, submersion and rising, caused something supernatural to happen.

First, when I went under the water, I purposefully identified with Christ when He died and was placed into a tomb. Symbolically, I was dying to self. In other words, when you're baptized, you identify with the truth, and that truth is that you have died to your old nature, to its sins and passions—you've died. Believe it!—"Or do you not know that as many of us as were baptized into Christ Jesus were *baptized into His death*" (Rom. 6:3). It's done!

Second, when I came up out of the water, just as Christ was resurrected, so was I! Resurrection into newness of life!—"Therefore we were buried with Him through baptism into death, that just as Christ was raised from the *dead by the glory* of the Father, even so we also should walk in newness of life" (Rom. 6:4). Done! A spiritual impartation happened; it was activated by the power of what was taking place in the spirit by that prophetic act.

Although we tend to put resurrection in the future, it isn't just a future event! When that revelation hit me, I started developing a resurrection mindset, thinking: *My spirit has been raised from the dead. I know what it's like, that same "glory" that raised Christ from the dead. That same glory is what's touched my spirit and made me alive! I've already experienced the very same resurrection power that raised Jesus up from the tomb; it not only has touched me, it's working inside of me! It's the anointing, the Holy Spirit that dwells in me!* That revelation was like being gloriously born again, again!

Being filled with the Spirit has always been a powerful key to the manifestation of power and anointing in my life and ministry, but I have to stay "juiced!" I often just soak in the reality of Romans 8:11 as I lay on my bed at night—it's so powerful!

How often I hear people say, "I need Todd to lay hands on me." For many, healing seems to be an outward thing. But God wants people to know that the healing anointing comes through the Spirit who dwells *in* you—that healing anointing is *in* you. The Holy Spirit isn't outside of you—healing isn't outside of you—it's where the Holy Spirit dwells—in you. God's trying to get your attention! He's saying, "You have that same Spirit—the same Spirit that raised Jesus from the dead lives in you right now! He's the very same Spirit who was there at the creation of the entire universe. He's the same Spirit who empowered the ministry of Jesus to heal all of those who were oppressed of the devil. He lives in you!"

Five minutes contemplating on that that reality and I'm in power—ready to go and believe for the impossible. The Holy Spirit wants us to have this Kingdom mindset. The Kingdom of Heaven is at hand, and the Kingdom of God is within you. Don't allow your mind to hold you back and put limitations on you. You can walk in your godly inheritance now. All that is holding you back is the limitation of your natural mind. You will begin to see the Kingdom of God at work when you learn to see with the eyes of faith.

Your miracles come from within. The healing anointing comes from within. If Jesus sits in heavenly places, at the right hand of God the Father, where does He live? He lives in you. Christ in you, the hope of glory (see Col 1:27). The heavenly places are in you, and your heart is the door.

Your mind should be on the Father and on getting to know Him through the precious Holy Spirit. Jesus knew this when He gave us the model prayer, a manner of praying in a quiet place whereby we come to know Him.

Within this model, as I wrote in my introduction, Jesus essentially teaches us the basics of welcoming God's world into our world—the heavenly realm into our realm here on earth. We are to worship and praise Him, surrender ourselves completely to Him, repent and seek forgiveness of sin, and forgive others and declare His power and His Kingdom and His glory forever.

The Truth of His Word for Faith

The Holy Spirit wants us to receive a Kingdom mindset now. Remember, it's not just about a future Kingdom. That is part of it, yes, but the Kingdom of Heaven is at hand, and the Kingdom of God is within you now, here. The Kingdom of God is on earth as it is in Heaven. The truth of His Word will give you faith to believe that it is God's will for you to experience Heaven every day.

I know that I've come to such a place of Kingdom consciousness that I am living in my inheritance of Heaven now. I'm not waiting only for the future. I am dreaming dreams and having visions, I am seeing the lame walk and the deaf hear, I am prophesying, and I am experiencing the reality of the supernatural realm of God, here on earth, right now! The Kingdom of Heaven is at hand. When we look at the world and its system, we have to understand that the kingdoms of this world have become the kingdoms of our Lord and Christ (see Rev. 11:15). It's done! The world just doesn't know it yet! The knowledge of the glory of the Lord is released through us as sons and daughters of God. We're dispensers of His glory that cause His Kingdom to come on earth as it is in Heaven.

When we manifest the anointing, we release it! God wants us to know who we're called to be, and He wants us to walk in the *fullness* of what He has intended for us and what is ours. When we do, we'll be a company of people who manifest Heaven so much that cities and whole nations will be impacted by Heaven's Gospel.

Listen, certainly God wants His will done on earth as it is in Heaven. He wants to partner with us and show us Heaven's realities so that they will be real on earth. When your partnership with God is at that co-laboring level with Him, so that heaven and earth converge, your whole life in Christ will take on a whole new meaning! Ponder that!

God is huge! He wants us to live our lives "out of the box" just as He does. How will the world know who He is if we don't look like Him? He'll display His glory through us, but we need to get with it—we must find out what God wants us to do, see what He's doing, and really do it!

In Moses' day, the magicians had occult power, big time. Had Moses failed to recognize and walk in God's power, had he just tried to take on Pharaoh and his magicians with a "let's try and take a good stab at it" attitude, would he have displayed the might of God's glory? Would the fear of God have come? Recall that God told Moses to *tell* Pharaoh that He would display His power so that the whole nation of Egypt would see that there was no other God like Him, that His fame would spread throughout the earth (see Exod. 9:14-16). Listen. How will the world see God's power and majesty—how will the nations be won to Christ—unless we, that's you and me, get serious and boldly demonstrate who He really is?

Before every meeting and sometimes for days and days, I spend time with the Lord—and I ask to see what the Father is doing. Often, He shows me, and I can boldly declare what He has shown me right at the start of the meeting. Whether it's someone who will be healed of deafness, or someone freed of addiction, I can boldly declare the works of the Lord because I have seen Him heal them.

The hour demands that we glorify Him in the earth, but if we're not manifesting Him to the world, it will not be changed. We have to surrender our lives completely to God, get seriously down on our knees, and become consecrated vessels as the Body of Christ—the company of believers marked and seared with the presence of the Holy Spirit—marked because we look like Jesus.

How much of God can you receive and manifest in your flesh? What's keeping you from more: the natural, carnal mind, the limitations of the flesh, distractions, busyness, and the world? Those things will try to prevent and keep you from manifesting His fullness and Kingdom fullness in your life.

Having a Kingdom mindset has everything to do with God's love being revealed and His glory being released in the earth. A lost and dying humanity need the saving knowledge of the Lord Jesus Christ. "And how shall they believe in Him of whom they have not heard? And how shall they hear without a preacher" (Rom. 10:14). So I ask, how will they hear unless we go anointed and empowered with a divinely inspired Kingdom mindset?

Press in to know the Lord. If you'll pursue Him with all of your heart, you'll have a true Kingdom mindset, anointed and empowered to go and do the work in Jesus' name.

PERSONAL PRAYER

Father, today I pray that You would release to me into a greater reality and a greater understanding of the Kingdom that is within me and that I can carry it into the lost and dying world, expanding and advancing

Your Kingdom here on earth. Please help me to begin to see that every place that I go, I carry Heaven with me that the world may be redeemed and saved. As I understand Heaven and what it's like there—having no sickness or disease, poverty or lack—I want to learn how to take the earth for Your glory, Lord. Thank You that Your Kingdom has come. Give me a revelation of who I am as a carrier of Heaven in me, because I want to be a blessing everywhere You lead me and to see people transformed and impacted by Your Spirit. Reveal to me those things that keep me from experiencing more of You— those things that prevent me from manifesting more of Your power in my flesh, more of the fullness of You. Bring me to that place of Kingdom consciousness so that I can live my inheritance now. Please give me a Kingdom mindset. It's so awesome that the same Spirit that raised Jesus from the dead lives in me and that by that same Spirit You quicken and bring life to my mortal flesh. Thank You for conveying me from the kingdom of darkness to the Kingdom of light. Because You love the Son, I have faith to see and know that You will show me all things. Give me a revelation of Your love and of who I am as Your child so that I can experience life on earth as it is in Heaven now.

"Your Kingdom come" is inviting God's world into our world so that the earth begins to take on the image and the nature of "as it is in Heaven" now. As you invite the Kingdom and the Kingdom begins to manifest in your presence, defeat turns into victory, sickness into healing, and disease into miracles. So welcome the realm of Heaven into your life. What it looks like in Heaven now is what you should desire for your life, your church, your city, and your nation.

KEY KINGDOM PRINCIPLES

- Hunger for God. Pursue Him.

- Ask for revelation of Jesus and of the Holy Spirit in your life.

- Pray for the baptism of the Holy Spirit, if you haven't yet received this awesome gift.

- Welcome the Kingdom as Christ modeled it. Pray that it would be on earth for you as it is in Heaven now.

- Seek an intimate relationship and communion with God through intimacy, soaking, worship.

- Ask God for revelation of who you are in Him, and of Who He is in you.

- Surrender your will, lay down your life, and die to self.

Endnotes

1. The Bible refers to it as the Kingdom of Christ, the Kingdom of Christ and of God, the Kingdom of David, the Kingdom, and the Kingdom of Heaven. All denote the same thing under different aspects, such as Christ's authority and rule on the earth, the blessings and advantages that would flow from this rule, and the Church (the collective subjects of the Kingdom).

2. Barton W. Johnson, "Commentary on John 1," *The People's New Testament* (1891), http://www.studylight.org/com/pnt/view .cgi?book=joh&chapter=001 (accessed 1 August 2007).

CHAPTER 2

THE GOSPEL OF THE KINGDOM

The Gospel of the Kingdom is the Gospel of power. It is a Gospel of cause and effect! In this chapter, you'll discover the power that is in the Gospel of the Kingdom and why miracles must happen. Discover how the power of the Gospel of the Kingdom releases signs and wonders as you go out to proclaim God's "Kingdom come" to the captive. Learn how to witness with boldness and strength, overcoming fears or reticence. Be filled with faith and power through confidence in the Gospel and in "God with us." Finally, it is my heart that you receive impartation and release into the ministry of miracles.

THE GOSPEL ACCORDING TO PAUL

God doesn't want us to walk in darkness, but rather to walk with our spiritual eyes wide open so that we can see what He is saying and doing in Heaven. Jesus made this possible through the redemptive power of the Cross. Because of His sacrifice, He opened the

Kingdom for all believers to minister and function as He did, in the power and the anointing of the Holy Spirit.

If you can get a revelation of this verse penned by Paul, you will see miracles, because the revelation of the Gospel is the revelation of the *arm of the Lord* (see Isa. 53:1). *Power* went along with the *word of Christ* to heal, save, and deliver.

> *For I am not ashamed of the gospel of Christ, for it is the power of God to salvation for everyone who believes, for the Jew first and also for the Greek* (Romans 1:16).

The Gospel of God is the power of God! The Gospel *without* power is *not* the Gospel of Jesus Christ. Jesus always connected the Kingdom and the Gospel together. The Kingdom is the creative power of God taken out of the heavens into an earthly scene for a supernatural release of miracles.

If you hear the good news of Jesus Christ preached but don't see people saved, healed, delivered, or transformed, you're not hearing the full Kingdom Gospel. Sadly, our gospel today, for the most part, has become one of "I think," or "In my opinion," and even, "If you'd like to believe with me, this is what I think." Thank goodness the Word of the Lord never returns void (see Isa. 55:10-11). Many in the Body of Christ have sacrificed the Gospel of power for the gospel of political correctness, a gospel that doesn't upset the order for the day, or a sterile one with no depth, reality, or wonder-working power. Consequently, many churches are empty, dry, or filled with thirsty, sick, dying, desperate people.

"I am not ashamed of the gospel" reveals Paul's heart to the sophisticated Romans. He likely wrote this because some there in the higher echelons might be embarrassed or too prideful to be known as followers of Jesus Christ who was crucified for their sins, especially since the lower castes were embracing the good news. Paul wasn't ashamed. He boldly said, "For it is the *power of God* to salvation for *everyone* who believes," because he knew that the good news of Jesus Christ has inherent power and that everyone—young, old, poor, and rich—needed Jesus. This Paul knew by experience because he had seen the dynamite (*dunamis*) power of God at work. *We* don't give the Gospel power, but *we can stop hindering* God's power by effectively preaching and demonstrating the *dunamis* Gospel of Christ.

When the disciples went about preaching the good news, it was more than a news flash. It had power! Every word of it had power. It wasn't advice on how people could lift their spirits. It was powerful enough to lift their spirits. It wasn't a "Ten Steps to Healing Thyself" program. The message itself could heal even the vilest of diseases. The Gospel doesn't bring power because it *is* power. It is God the Creator's power.[1] It is the Holy Spirit working through the Word, and without His power, the Gospel is but a folded newspaper. The power of God's Word will give a person the faith to entrust his or her whole life to Jesus in a heartbeat.

> *For the Word of God is living and powerful, and sharper than any two-edged sword, piercing even to the division of soul and spirit, and of joints and marrow, and is a discerner of the thoughts and intents of the heart* (Hebrews 4:12).

Paul had to have confidence in the power of the Gospel even to preach it or encourage others to preach it to the Romans because Rome thought it knew all about power. But for all the power they boasted about and thought they had as the world's powerhouse empire of the day, for all of their power, they were unable to turn away from their "cesspools of iniquity."[2] Like all of us, they were powerless to make themselves righteous before God. Such is the everlasting and mighty power of the Gospel of the Kingdom—that the Gospel of Jesus lives. Note that the power of the Roman Empire is long gone. Heaven and earth will pass away, but God's word will "by no means pass away" (Matt. 24:35).

CAUSE AND EFFECT

Words, words, words! We're inundated with words every day through television, the radio, the newspapers, self-help books, magazines, sermons, seminars, conferences, school, and so on. What the world doesn't need are more words that don't carry power. What it does need is the power and truth found in the words of the Gospel: the power for miracles, the power for awesome signs from God, the power for healings, and the power for freedom from oppression; but most of all, it needs the power to change minds, to change hearts, and to change lives. The world needs the invading, life-changing, transforming power of the Gospel of Jesus by the Holy Spirit.

The Gospel transformed the lives of the Christians of Thessalonica. Paul said, "For our Gospel did not come to you in word only, but also in power, and in the Holy Spirit and in much assurance..." (1 Thess. 1:5).

If the greatest preacher in the world preached the Gospel to a stadium filled with people, but the Holy Spirit didn't work through the Word, the preacher's words would be as empty as every other word we hear, because there'd be no power in the message. The Holy Spirit works through the Word *for cause and effect*, that everyone who hears the good news would receive power and life and thus experience life-changing transformation. With the Holy Spirit working through the Word, we can preach the Gospel of Jesus Christ with assurance, confidence, and boldness and see instant results.

What happened when the Thessalonians heard the Gospel of power? They became followers (see Thess. 1:6). They did an about-face and stopped following dead things. Yes, they were afflicted and would become even more afflicted by following Christ. Nevertheless, Paul had confidence in the power of God, and he knew where he was going, and they followed his lead. They received the good news even when it came with hardship. They received it joyfully, with the joy of the Holy Spirit! Then, like Paul, they themselves became examples to other believers (see Thess. 1:7).

This is exactly how Kingdom work should happen. Even though the Thessalonians had only followed Jesus a short time, they were examples of Christ's love and power. This is what the world needs— this working of the Holy Spirit through the Word. The power of the Gospel and the Holy Spirit fueling it makes us bold witnesses. It is our work to show the world Christianity, to live it, demonstrate it, and not just talk about it. When that happens, when the Body of believers boldly witness, the world will talk about it. Think front page headlines, top-of-the news hour!

News of the Thessalonians' transformation spread like wildfire. (Thessalonica was a major commercial center that people traveled to for trade and so on, so news traveled fast.) Paul said, "From you the word of the Lord has sounded forth" (Thess. 1:8a). In that context, it meant that the words that they preached were like a trumpet blast! It wasn't long before the entire region had heard about their works.

Imagine what would happen in the marketplace of today if we, as the people of Thessalonica did, would sound forth the Gospel of power. Can you imagine how far and fast that trumpet would sound to the nations?

Faith and Impact

"Your faith toward God has gone out, so that we do not need to say anything" (Thess. 1:8b). The Word of the Lord sounded forth, and their faith had gone out. Here we see cause and effect again in faith and impact. For faith to happen, we have to experience that Gospel of power for ourselves; it has to impact us before it will impact others. When it impacts us, our faith and boldness rise in us to spread the Word. Not only that, but just our lives as witnesses and living testaments of the glory and power of the Lord to transform will cause murmuring, wonder, curiosity, and interest. Christ's words to the woman at the well caused her to run into town and tell everyone, "Come see this Man who knows things about me that I never told Him" (see John 4:29).

The Gospel of Jesus Christ is not just a message. Yes, the message is true that Jesus came, He died, and He rose again, and that God so loved the world that He gave His only begotten Son. Yes, there's a message in that, but Jesus didn't just deliver a message. He *demonstrated* the message, and so did Paul "in mighty signs and wonders, by the power of the Spirit of God, so that from Jerusalem and round about to Illyricum I have fully preached the Gospel of Christ" (Rom. 15:19).

Hold Fast the Pattern of Sound Words

In his message to sometimes-timid Timothy, Paul said, "Therefore do not be ashamed of the testimony of our Lord, nor of me His prisoner, but share with me in the sufferings for the Gospel according to the *power* of God" (2 Tim. 1:8).

Have we immunized the Gospel from spreading? Do we sanitize its message so as not to offend? Do we sugarcoat it to make it more palatable? Are we afraid of rejection? Mocking? Persecution? Paul said, "*Hold fast* the pattern of sound words which you have heard from me, in faith and love which are in Christ Jesus" (2 Tim. 1:13). Do we hold back the pattern of faith and love because of fear? Paul said, "For God has not given us a spirit of fear, but of power and of love and of a sound mind" (2 Tim. 1:7). In other words, "Don't be afraid to suffer, Timothy, because God's power will see you through it. Remain in His perfect pattern of words and you won't be afraid."

All of those things—power, love, and a sound mind—we have inherited in Christ Jesus. These are all things we need to guide us as we proclaim the Gospel of the Kingdom.

Just as in Paul's day, the message to follow Christ and make Him Lord and Savior over everything seems strange to many—perhaps even more so in our "I'll do it myself" world. The plan of God in

Christ Jesus may seem foolish. For some, it may expose them as being "weak" or may even cause them fear, but Paul knew that the message of salvation was the living and active power of God to transform and save. There was no way Paul would be ashamed of it or afraid of it. There was no way he *wouldn't* preach the Gospel of power to anyone lost or captive—be it someone influential and powerful or someone (in the world's eyes) unimportant and insignificant. He told Timothy as much, and we should take care to heed his wise counsel.

> *For this reason I also suffer these things; nevertheless I am not ashamed, for I know whom I have believed and am persuaded that He is able to keep what I have committed to Him until that day* (2 Timothy 1:12).

THE CHRIST OF POWER

How can we call ourselves Christians—followers of Christ Jesus—if we don't follow the Christ of power? That's who He is! How can we not believe that miracles, signs, and wonders are for today? To say that miracles passed away with the age of the disciples is to say that the Gospel has passed away too. It's to say that Jesus didn't really die and rise again for *us* and that the same Spirit that raised Him from the dead doesn't really live inside of us. It would be a powerless spirit—not the Holy Spirit—because He is unchanging just as God is unchanging, just as Jesus is the same yesterday, today, and forever (see Heb. 13:8). Has the Bible persuaded you that He is able?

We can preach the Gospel all day long, but that won't win souls. That won't win the hearts of the people. We can talk, try to theorize, theologize, reason, argue, debate, and spend time trying to prove that Jesus lived, but that won't win a heart. How often do we see the religious mindset that believes that the more Scripture quoting, the more yelling, the more hell fire and brimstone preaching, the greater the chance to win someone over for the Kingdom? Likewise, how often do we see people sitting or standing there listening in stone-cold silence or indifference?

My team and I, on one of our visits to South Africa, did some open-air power preaching in the ghettos of one town. We saw many drug addicts and gangsters coming to know the Jesus of power, and many fell out under the power of the Holy Spirit and came to know the Savior. But just behind us on a hill were about 30 gangsters taunting and mocking these people. I called out to them and said, "You don't believe all this?"

Several replied, "No, we don't believe this, we don't believe in God! It's all fake and staged."

What could I do? How could I convince them? Would preaching more convince them? Would a lesson in theology convince these violent youth and drug addicts? I thought not. I called them over and said, "Fine, that's what you believe, but line up right here and let me lay hands on you. Watch how God will touch you. I guarantee that if God doesn't touch you, that I will say that God isn't real."

They lined up and the Holy Spirit smacked them, my friends! Whoosh. Down they all went, laid out under His power, and every one of them got saved. That is why we need a manifestation of the demonstration of the Spirit of God and power. That's power evangelism! When we combine it with the prophetic, it's even more so.

FAITH FORWARD INTO THE FIELD

These days, especially in North America, we have "heard it all." Christianity doesn't stand out—it's grouped with every other thing that claims it can change, transform, fix, or alter. Some people even consider our faith hypocritical because they don't see what we claim when we witness. We preach "I am the Lord that healeth thee" (Exod. 15:26 KJV), but how many healings do we see? If we preach, "By His stripes, you are healed" (Isa. 53:5; 1 Pet. 2:4), but don't step out and lay hands on a person, or pray for that person, how is that going to win him or her? Do we really have faith that God heals? Does fear hold us back? What's holding you back? Why say, "I'll keep you in my prayers," when you can pray on the spot, believing that what you ask for God will deliver? We have to get off the platform and into the midst of the people with the hands-on Gospel of truth! We have hundreds of promises, but do we ever venture forth with them? God doesn't lie. He's unchangeable, and His promises pierce the present just as they broke through in the past.

PLATFORM OR DEMONSTRATION?

Is Christianity more of a platform of promises, or do we actually go into the midst of people with God's promises and demonstrate them—His promises to heal and deliver, to bind and loose, and to save and set free? How often do we use Christianity more as a platform to grow our churches for something rather than as a tool to win the lost? The winning of the lost to Christ through mighty demonstrations of His power is platform enough. Armed with the truth, we speak His promises into the lost, into the sick, into the dying, into the captive: "By His stripes, *you are healed* in the name of Jesus Christ of Nazareth!" Lay hands on someone and say, "Jesus said, 'Behold, I have come that you might have life and have it more abundantly'" (see John 10:10). Everything people need, want, or desire they can find in Him.

The power of God operating through us will open dull, apathetic, and hardened ears and hearts. The only thing that is going to release a powerhouse of harvest is the Kingdom of power in us and through us. We are living in a time of acceleration, my friends. Time is short, and it is going to have to be a demonstration of the Kingdom of Heaven at hand. God is anointing and gifting His people to witness and preach the Gospel of power with the power of the Holy Spirit. I tell you, I make sure that in my meetings people know that God is real and in their midst.

Christians need encounters with God. It sounds silly, doesn't it? When we accepted Jesus into our lives, wouldn't we think that His coming to live in us is an encounter? But it's not until we turn that into communion and fellowship with Him—two-way dialogue and spending time in His presence, time in the Spirit, and truly pursuing Him—that we're truly encountering Him.

LAY HOLD OF HIM

We must lay hold of Him if we are to see what He is doing in Heaven! How can we bring Heaven to earth if we don't even have a sense of God's character? My friends, let go of "head" Christianity and embrace relationship Christianity. Relationship with God is explosive and dynamite. Can you imagine actually being able to *see* what the Father in Heaven is doing? Jesus did. He admitted that "the Son can do nothing of Himself, but what He sees the Father do; for whatever He does, the Son also does in like manner" (John 5:19). This was key to His Kingdom ministry. Here Jesus is saying, "My Dad's been working, so I've been working!" What a powerful truth. Could it be that Jesus saw visions of the Father performing miracles and then He emulated the Father's example? Did He see the Father heal the lame or open blind eyes? Did He see the Father raise Lazarus from the dead? Did God first bring in a great haul of fish with His net, or did He first multiply the loaves and the fishes? I'm certain Jesus knew how to calm the wind and the seas because of the Father's ability.

How can you apply this? Suppose we're conducting a crusade. Because God lives outside of time, the meeting we will hold tomorrow has already happened in the realm of eternity and predestination—it's already been lived out in Heaven! Our job in ministry is to see, to wait, to listen, and to understand what the Father is doing in Heaven and to replicate it on earth. This is His will being done on earth as it is in Heaven.

The day before a group of our interns left to do some power evangelism work on a university campus in Bellingham, Washington, one of the interns had a prophetic dream. He dreamt of a large man with a leg injury, wearing a boot cast. In the dream, the intern saw himself praying for the man and the man being healed. The following day, he walked around campus keeping an eye out for this man he saw in his dream. Success! There he was! He went up to him and said, "I had a dream about you. In it, I prayed for you and you got healed! Strange as it seems, I dreamt about you, and here you are!"

The fellow shared that he was an all-state pro linebacker and had suffered an injury. The doctor told him he would be in the cast for as long as six more weeks. Once the man wrapped his mind around the odd offer of prayer and felt more comfortable with it, the intern prayed. Right away, this linebacker was healed. He kicked off his boot and ran around to prove it! God has been busy working, and it's our turn to get working to synchronize Heaven and earth. We see what the Father does, and we do what the Father does.

Scripture shows us that God has worked this way before. God gave Moses a pattern to work from to build a tabernacle for Him. Why did He do that? Because if Moses followed God's pattern exactly, then the glory would surely come. Moses built a replica on earth of the true heavenly temple. It had to be done to exacting detail, reproduced to precise measurements. Only then would God's glory come and fill it. Many of us are not seeing a greater dimension of God's glory and power because we haven't learned how to see what the Father is doing and we don't know how He wants it done.

By faith we understand that the worlds were framed by the word of God, so that the things which are seen were not made of things which are visible (Hebrews 11:3).

Everything that I have today is because I began to "build it" out of the heavens. I began to "frame it out" with the Word of God based on what God promised me, based on every dream, every prophetic word, every promise, every Scripture, every desire. I framed it out based on what I had in my heart, based on who I am and what I am called to do. I got into that spirit, I got into that invisible place, and I purposed myself like this: "Everything that is in this realm, God made out of a place that is invisible, so I am going to use the invisible to build the visible." That's biblical.

HE'LL PULL BACK THE CURTAIN

I always wait on God and seek to see what He is doing, often hours before I even minister. I ask the Holy Spirit to pull back the curtain and let me "live out" the miracles He wants to do in that service before I get there. God wants to communicate with all of us in this way if we will just take the time to wait in His presence and see what He is doing. These times of waiting on God are incredibly intense experiences for me. The Lord may give me ten specific words of knowledge for people who will be in the service that evening, but I know that if I had waited longer, it could have been 20 or 30. The longer you wait in God's presence, the more revelation He will pour out. I've come to the place where, the longer I wait in God's presence, the more incredible the details I receive are. Often I'll live out the service in my mind as God lets me "see" and "hear" in the spirit. I sometimes hear those who will be there talk to each other about their hope for healing, the type of sickness they have, and so on. Later I may even know their names, and I usually can tell them what ails them, with precision.

I received an invitation once to minister in Kansas City at a huge (4,000 attendees) signs, wonders, and miracles crusade, alongside of several great prophets of the day. It was my first time ministering alongside of the likes of these great saints of God, and I found it a tad intimidating because I was the new kid on the proverbial block.

Things were well underway when I arrived several days after the conference started; however, there had not yet been a manifestation of signs, wonders, or miracles, even with the lineup of anointed speakers. It seemed odd, given the topics of the coming healing revival, supernatural ministry, and the function of miracles, but for whatever reason, God chose to wait.

I'm sure people started to wonder why they hadn't yet witnessed a demonstration of even one miracle, sign, or wonder. It would be like going to a prophetic conference and not hearing any prophecy. As it turns out, these great colleagues of mine felt that they would leave it all to me, and in fact, everyone anticipated my arrival: "Well, Todd is coming in on Saturday, so I guess that's when the miracle part of this conference will happen." Can you imagine the pressure on me? I went back to my hotel room until it was my turn to speak, and I called out to the Lord: "Oh God, give me strategy! What's happening in Heaven, Father? What am I going to be doing tonight? What's the message? Help me!"

As I lay on my bed awaiting His answers, He said to me, "Todd, tonight you are going to move in the word of knowledge."

I answered, "Oh no I'm not."

"Oh yes you are, Todd. In fact, you are going to give the most accurate detailed words you have ever given!"

"But God," I replied with surprise, "I'm not *moving* in the word of knowledge tonight! Let others do it that have done it for a long time, but not *me!* Why can't You let me just go in and preach the Word and pray for the sick?"

"Todd, you are moving in the word of knowledge," He said. And that was that, until suddenly God gave me a vision in the spirit right there in my hotel room. Even though the meeting was still five hours away, there I was "in the service," overhearing a conversation between an usher and a couple. They were asking the usher if he could arrange for me to lay hands on them, but the usher told them that it wasn't possible, that I was up front already and that he couldn't disturb me.

But the man was adamant and said, "No! You have to tell Todd that we've come here all the way from Mexico! I'm a pastor and this is my wife. There is a boy in our home church who was hit by a car and went into a coma. He's out of it now, but it has affected him and we want Todd to lay hands on us for his miracle."

That's where my vision ended. I awoke, got dressed, and left the room for my meeting. The conference room was packed and filled with worshipers. Once on the platform, I immediately asked, "Where are the pastor and his wife from Mexico, the ones with the boy at their church hit by a car, who's now out of a coma?"

The couple flew forward to the platform. "That's us," they shouted, "How did you know?"

I simply replied, "The boy will be healed."

They then explained the extent of the boy's problems, and suddenly I wasn't too sure of things. They explained how the boy was now not only a quadriplegic; he was also in a vegetative state.

Thanks a lot, Lord, I thought. *I've already opened my mouth and prophesied that he will be healed, but I didn't know it was that severe.*

This is why God often doesn't let us in on the finer details—because sometimes it causes nerves or doubt. It's a little like Peter getting out of the boat to walk on water. He was fine until the realization of what he was doing hit him. He realized, "Hold on there a second, I'm *on* water!" Would I have had such confidence had I known the extent of the boy's situation?

Let me ask you a question: should these kinds of miracles that blow apart our expectations of God be occasional spikes or highlights in our walk that we only experience occasionally, or should they be happening all the time? What is your expectation? Would you like God to move powerfully through you in everything?

How often do you expect to hear God speak to you with absolute clarity? If the Father loves the Son and shows Him all that He does, why can't God show us, who are in Christ, what He is doing? (See John 6:20.) God wants to show us *all* that He is doing. Do we only have faith to see or hear God once a year…once a month …or more frequently? If you truly have a revelation of the Father's love for you—that you are a beloved son or a daughter—then you won't expect to see Him only once a month or even once a week. The Father loves Jesus and shows Him all things that He does. God doesn't do miraculous things once in a while—He's busy, so why aren't you busy doing the Father's business?

Don't worry—asking God what He's up to won't bother Him one bit. You can live in the truth of "I can do what I see God doing" and practice it daily!

KINGDOM HELPS

Overcome the Spirit of Fear (See 2 Timothy 1:7; Luke 12:32; and Romans 8:15.)

- Seek revelation of Emmanuel, God with Us.

- God will confirm the Word through accompanying signs (see Mark 16:20).

- The Lord will work with you; He'll be alongside of you.

- Don't fear; He's already "there" waiting for you.

- Respond to His calling, and He'll begin His work.

- We are His ambassadors: authority, power, and angels are our backup.

- You and God are partners. Partners work together. You cannot work without God.

Develop Confidence

The ministry of the Kingdom of God is the bringing of creative power out of the heavens to override the natural and the impossible in the earth and release the supernatural power of God. Take time to study and ponder the following Scripture verses: Matthew 12:28; Mark 1:15; 4:26; 9:1; and Luke 4:43; 8:1; 9:2; 11:20; 17:21.

Signs, Wonders, and Miracles Are Released:

- as we go out into the world (see Mark 16:15,17).

- as we come out of our comfort zone (see Rom. 1:16).

- as we overcome the spirit of fear (see Rom. 8:15).

- as we reach out to our neighbors (see Rom. 13:9; Matt. 19:19; 22:39).

- as we reach out to touch the sick, the captive, the unsaved (see Matt. 10:8).

- as we go into the hospitals, prisons, and streets with the reality of the Holy Spirit (see Rom. 15:13; Acts 10:38).

Personal Prayer

Father God, forgive me for those times I have not come out of my comfort zone to boldly preach Your Gospel, which is power to do the impossible. I want the boldness to preach the Gospel of the Kingdom for cause and effect and faith and impact. I want to move forward in faith, advancing Your Kingdom through mighty demonstrations of Your promise that it is Your will that all are healed. Father, I want to bring in the harvest with Your Word, and Your Word only. Help me to hold fast to the sound pattern of Your words, and may Your Word sound forth through me by the power of Your Spirit. In Jesus' mighty name I pray, amen!

Endnotes

1. David Guzik, "Commentary on Romans 1," *David Guzik's Commentaries* on the Bible (Enduring Word Media, 1997-2003), http://www.studylight.org/com/guz/view.cgi?book=ro&chapter= 001 (accessed 24 June 2008).

2. Seneca, the ancient philosopher.

CHAPTER 3

DEMONSTRATION OF THE KINGDOM

Most people think they have to learn how to move in the anointing, but it's not something one learns. I can teach you about the anointing, but I can't help you move in it. Nobody taught me how to move in it. I didn't have someone sit down and teach me for hours about what I had to do. Neither did your pastor for that matter.

Do you know what happened to me? The Holy Spirit. That's right! God visited me, and for three months, I had encounter after encounter with Him. All I did was about Jesus. All I practiced was the presence of God. I hungered for encounters with Him. If I had one, I wanted another. Never satisfied, I wanted God to get a hold of me, and I tell you, I wanted a hold of Him!

The more time I hung out with the Spirit of God, the more the Spirit rubbed off on me. The more the Spirit rubbed off on me, the more I carried His power and glory into even my own church and world. Literally hanging out with God—that is, being in His presence—gets His glory and the substance of Heaven all over you so that when you go about your business you're bringing Heaven to earth in mighty demonstrations of God's power. Remember Moses' face as he came down that mountain (see Exod. 34:29)? That glory glowed off of him—in and through him. He came down with the substance of Heaven smeared all over his face. You need a God encounter my friend—the Spirit of God upon you—and when that happens, you will receive power to be His witness (see Acts 1:8).

GET EXCITED ABOUT HIS POWER

Woven into the message of the Gospel and evangelism is the power of God: "As you go, preach, saying 'The kingdom of heaven is at hand'" (Matt. 10:7). If there is no Spirit of God upon us, there's no power. If there's no power, there's no going. If there's no power and Spirit of the Lord upon us, there's no drive, motivation, confidence, zeal, boldness, courage, or persuasion to say, "My God, I want harvest!" Without the anointing, there's no thrust on repentance, on calling backsliders back to God, or on going into the ghettos with the demonstration of the power of God. There's just staleness.

Listen: God doesn't give miracles for showmanship or for your good name. He doesn't give miracles for a good meeting so that a ministry can grow. He gives miracles because He's moved with compassion. Miracles demonstrate to a lost and dying world the power of God, the God of love, to save, heal, and deliver even the lowest of the low.

I guarantee you that the more we take the Gospel of Jesus Christ into the streets, the more we'll experience increase of the manifestation of the power of God. God always blesses soul-winning. He'll always bless you as you go out and preach "the Kingdom of Heaven is at hand." He says, "As you go...heal the sick, cleanse the lepers, raise the dead, cast out demons. Freely you have received, freely give (Matt. 10:7-8)." Go into the world—these signs and wonders will follow you.

I am excited about going into the world—into the drug houses and prisons, into the orphanages and old age homes, into the hospitals and sanatoriums, into the cities and nations. I can't wait until tomorrow. Why? Because I am excited about the power of God! For goodness sake, why preach the Gospel in church where most are already saved? We've heard it—it's time we started demonstrating it *in* the world, where God meant it to be. Why else would Jesus say, "As you go"? Go already! We have the power of the Gospel and the presence of the Holy Spirit. What more do we need?

GOSPEL = MIRACLES

Do you know what I love about the Gospel? The fact that miracles are joined to it—they are both welded firmly together just as the Holy Spirit and the crucified Christ are one. That's why we hear references to the Spirit of Christ (see Rom. 8:9). The Holy Spirit and God the Father are one—that's why we hear references to the Spirit of God.[1] As such, we cannot separate the Holy Spirit, who manifests the power of the Kingdom of God, from the Gospel. The Gospel is the dynamic presence of the Holy Spirit. He was a part of everything that Jesus did. Christ wasn't even born without the Holy Spirit, because Mary was "found with child of the Holy Spirit" before she and Joseph even experienced intimacy together (see Matt. 1:18).

Christ didn't minister without the Holy Spirit. He didn't even die on the Cross without Him. Jesus "through the eternal Spirit offered Himself without spot to God," and Jesus didn't even rise from the dead without the Holy Spirit (see Heb. 9:14).

The ministry of the Holy Spirit is to bring people to a revelation of Jesus Christ, the Spirit of Christ. When Silas and Timothy had come from Macedonia, Paul was compelled *by the Spirit* and testified to the Jews that Jesus is the Christ (see Acts 18:5).

Everything's wrapped together—the Holy Spirit and the Gospel, the Holy Spirit and Calvary, the Holy Spirit and the death and resurrection of Jesus. Paul often intertwined and wove references to each member of the Trinity in his letters and ministry—he couldn't even talk about God without recognizing His three persons! In Romans, he says, "Now I beg you, brethren, through the Lord Jesus Christ, and through the love of the Spirit, that you strive together with me in prayers to God for me" (Rom. 15:30). In Second Corinthians, he says, "The grace of the Lord Jesus Christ, and the love of God, and the communion of the Holy Spirit be with you all" (2 Cor. 13:14).

Do you want to see more power than you can shake a stick at when you preach or speak of Jesus Christ? Do you want to release that Gospel with miracles, healings, signs, and wonders? I know you do. Take a cue from Paul and preach all three persons of the Trinity in the Gospel. Talk about power. Whoa!

WORD AND DEED

In Paul's ministry, especially to the Gentiles, God used mighty signs and wonders and the broader power of the Spirit of God to help Paul *fully* preach the Gospel of Christ everywhere he went. He said, "I fully preached the Gospel of Christ" (see Rom. 15:19). Anything less would be bare and depthless preaching, that is, without the miraculous and active work of the Holy Spirit more than evident. Do you know that Paul traveled and spread the Gospel far away in Illyricum, which is modern-day Yugoslavia and Albania? It spread far and wide—by the power of the Holy Spirit. He loved to pioneer. He preferred that, in fact, to building on someone else's foundation—not because it was wrong, but because there was so much to do. He loved to preach and break new territory for the Gospel, to present it in new places (see Rom. 15:20-21). He had reason to glory in Christ Jesus in the things that pertained to God and in the things that Christ accomplished through him "in word and deed" (see Rom. 15:17-18). By Word and deed was how the evangelist Paul won souls.

THAT WE MIGHT MINISTER AS PRIESTS

Nevertheless, brethren, I have written more boldly to you on some points, as reminding you, because of the grace given to me by God, that I might be a minister of Jesus Christ to the Gentiles, ministering the gospel of God, that the offering of the Gentiles might be acceptable, sanctified by the Holy Spirit (Romans 15:15-16).

Nowhere else in the New Testament is the word *ministering*, used in the context it is used in the above verse, for it refers to a priestly service. Here Paul himself ministered, "acting like a priest," as it related to the conversion of the Gentiles as an acceptable sacrifice to God (see Heb. 7:11-28). So the ministry of the Gospel is really a mirror of the Old Testament priestly offering:

> *For if He were on earth, He would not be a priest, since there are priests who offer the gifts according to the law* (Hebrews 8:4).

> *Now when these things had been thus prepared, the priests always went into the first part of the tabernacle, performing the services* (Hebrews 9:6).

> *...and has made us kings and priests to His God and Father, to Him be glory and dominion forever and ever. Amen* (Revelation 1:6).

In Romans 15:17-20, Paul *glories* in the work that God has done *through* him. Do you have reason to glory in Christ Jesus over those things He has accomplished through you in word and deed? Have you fully preached or witnessed the Gospel of Christ? Do you minister as a priest?

PREACH POWER WITH A MESSAGE

Paul was not a man with a message. Paul was a man of power with a message. Filled with the Holy Spirit, he was imbued with power from on high and with a message. Are you a man or woman of power with a message? When the Holy Spirit fills you and anoints you with His power, that's when you'll preach the Gospel. That's when you'll be an effective witness. Paul himself attested that he would not have preached the Gospel if he hadn't done it for signs, wonders, and miracles. We all need a demonstration of the Spirit of God and power in our lives, and I believe He wants to impart that to you and to every believer.

Miracles are for today, and there's no harm in contending for them! I've had people "accuse" me of concentrating too much on the power of God to perform signs and wonders, and yet they say nothing about the doors the Lord opened up to me to preach in Africa to millions through the mediums of crusades, television, and radio broadcasting. They say nothing of the thousands of commitments to Christ in America and Canada alone over the years because of the tangible presence and power of God healing disease, taking away the pain of the suffering, and enabling the lame to walk, the blind to see, and the deaf to hear. They say, "Would you just forget the miracles? Enough already! Get to the message."

Hello?

If we as Spirit-filled believers do not walk in the fullness of what is available to us in salvation, then we *will* look hypocritical and dead. While all of the promises of God are yes and amen (see 2 Cor. 1:20) and God's Word remains sure (see 2 Pet. 1:19 KJV), how much more will a demonstration of His healing power bring people to Christ.

Sozo

If you're sick or suffering and not contending to get well by pressing in for a divine healing, then I might think that you don't understand the fullness of salvation: that salvation is for your *body*, soul, and spirit. *Sozo*. No, that doesn't mean that salvation is so-so. *Sozo* is a Greek word meaning to save, deliver, or protect (literally or figuratively); to heal, preserve, save (self), do well, be (or make) whole.

Receiving the revelation of *sozo* will not just impart to you faith to receive healing, but will impart the faith, confidence, and boldness to preach the *full* Gospel to all the nations. *Sozo* is the foundation of our faith for divine healing. It is salvation for the body, soul, and spirit *at the moment of salvation.*

There was no separation of salvation, healing, or deliverance in the ministry of Jesus. God sees spiritual redemption, deliverance, and physical healing as all needing the same remedy: salvation. The *sozo* context is used for "saved" (wholeness for the spirit) in Matthew 1:21, Acts 2:47, James 5:15, and Romans 10:9; for "saved" (wholeness for the soul—delivered) in Luke 8:36; and for "healed" (wholeness of the body) in Mark 5:34.

Could you ever tell a person that God doesn't want to save them? Do you believe that if anyone sincerely called on the Lord for mercy and forgiveness that He would save them? Why then do we have such difficulty believing that whoever calls upon the name of the Lord will be healed or delivered? We so readily accept salvation for our spirit yet resolve to live with sickness in our body, or affliction, or spiritual oppression. *Sozo* is the Gospel of power—it is God's willingness to save body, soul, and spirit all at once.

Just as much as Christ was wounded for our transgressions and iniquity, He also bore upon His body all of our afflictions so that by His stripes we are healed (see 1 Pet. 2:24). To take healings and miracles away from Calvary is to bring down the ministry of Jesus, the Gospel of God! To believe that we can have salvation but without power is to believe that Jesus never really rose from the dead and that there is no power in the Gospel. Yes, spread the word of Jesus Christ of Nazareth. Yes, there's infinite power in the Word—but theology alone won't save people if you're preaching power but don't believe in the power.

I tell you, when the power of God visits us, when we truly hunger for the anointing, when we have revelation of the immense power available to us, when we understand the fullness of salvation, when we believe everything about the Gospel, *then* we'll lay hands on the sick and they will recover. If more saints contended for that anointing, imagine whole cities taken in a day for Jesus! It doesn't matter who you are—big or small, young or old—if you hunger enough to know God and you're willing to dig into the Kingdom, our Sovereign God will sovereignly move through you in power for greater and greater works.

Listen, who's Todd Bentley? Who am I that God would use me, an ex-addict, a "nothing" in societal circles. Who am I? I am a man hungering after the One True God. I don't truly desire anything else but to know Him intimately! It's in that realm of seeking Him with all of my heart that everything else flows and comes into fullness. I can "hallelujah," and "amen" with the best of them, but if I don't know God, it's all empty.

I can't preach a Gospel of power if I don't believe in that power—and I believe—oh man I believe! I've seen His power. I've met Him; I've encountered Him; I've seen Him; I've been to Heaven; and it's all glorious!

If then you were raised with Christ, seek those things which are above, where Christ is, sitting at the right hand of God. Set your mind on things above, not on things on the earth. For you died, and your life is hidden with Christ in God. When Christ who is our life appears, then you also will appear with Him in glory (Colossians 3:1-4).

One time when I was in Atlanta, Georgia, moments before I was to preach, the Holy Spirit took me into a trance. Suddenly, I was traveling down a highway moving as fast as a car, but I wasn't in a vehicle! It was so real. I could see the cars and the pavement. The Lord told me to pay attention to the road signs because He was taking me somewhere. I saw a sign that said, "Chattanooga Highway," and took the exit. The next thing I knew, I was standing outside of a prison. Understand, I was still at the church—but in this vision I was somewhere else. As soon as I decided to go into the prison—bam—I was inside. As I walked through a cellblock, I knew I was headed toward a particular cell, and there met a young man who told me what he was in for. I shared the salvation message, and with renewed hope, He gave his life back to Jesus. Wow! When it was over, I asked God two questions. The first, "What do You want me to do with that experience—is something about to change or happen here in the earthly realm? He immediately answered me and told me that there was a woman in the very meeting I was about to preach in, there right now, who needed to hear what I had just seen and heard in that prison.

I shared every detail I could remember, the name of the exit, what the prison looked like, details about the man and our conversation. A woman jumped up and declared, "My best friend was supposed to be here tonight—but she's had an emergency. That's *her* son in that prison!"

I told her to get the woman on her cell phone. "Call her right now!" Talk about God's timing. At the very moment of our call, the woman told us that her other son was in the act of trying to kill his father. She was in total panic as she quickly shared how he was involved with witchcraft.

"Let's pray," I said. "I take authority over witchcraft and render it powerless in the name of Jesus!" Bam! Right then, something happened. The violence against the father stopped. A few hours later, the woman we'd called arrived at the meeting. She shared about that son and all of the details about what was happening at the moment we called. "As soon as you prayed that prayer," she said, "The assignment to kill his father stopped!"

If we are going to partner with God to overthrow the powers of darkness—because death and destruction stalk the earth continually—we have to have the anointing flowing out of our lives here on earth. We need the anointing that gives life—that empowers us to walk full-out in our authority, reigning, being determined believers who advance God's Kingdom in the earth just as it is in Heaven. The stakes are high, but resurrection power will make all the difference in the world.

IMMERSE YOURSELF IN HIM

You have no idea how greatly you can be used of God as you walk in the power of the Holy Spirit, but it takes hunger. Paul was hungry. He hungered and thirsted after God, and signs, wonders, and miracles followed his ministry. King David did too—and God gave him a kingdom.

To know the Holy Spirit, the Spirit of God, intimately is to know joy and power. Do you know what I love the most about the Holy Spirit? I love the fact that Jesus promised Him to us as the promise of the Father: "For John truly baptized with water, but you shall be baptized with the Holy Spirit not many days from now" (Acts 1:5). Salvation is precious and is a work of the Holy Spirit in regeneration. However, His work is not just an inner transformation of our new spiritual birth and sanctification; it is also the work of empowering believers as witnesses for Christ, thus fulfilling the Body of Christ's mission of Matthew 28 (see Matthew 28:18-20; Acts 1:8).

The act of being baptized is to be immersed or covered over in something. Jesus promised that the disciples would be immersed in the Holy Spirit. Little wonder, therefore, that following this, in His final teaching and promise before He ascended, He said to them, "But you *shall receive power* when the Holy Spirit has come upon you; and you shall be witnesses to Me in Jerusalem, and in all Judea and Samaria, and to the end of the earth" (Acts 1:8).

Witnessing to the far ends of the earth takes power, my friends—*sozo* power. Hey, they didn't have Lear jets and Hummers to get around in back in those days. Sandals and a donkey or camel was as good as it got. There wasn't the Internet or conference calling. Nix chat rooms and loud speakers. Forget television and radio. Yet, Jesus says that they shall witness everywhere. Witness what? Salvation of body, soul, and spirit—by the power of the Holy Spirit. Word of God power will spread through the demonstration of it, faster than the highest speed Internet service can transmit it.

MOVE IN MIRACLE POWER

The Holy Spirit is more than a speaking-in-tongues experience. It's more than the gifts of the Holy Spirit. It's more than being spiritually drunk in Him—(but I *especially* love that). The Holy Spirit is about *moving* in miracle power. When the disciples were first filled, they moved in power—such as the healing of a lame man at the Temple Beautiful—and the Lord added to the church daily (see Acts 3:1-10). However, jump over to Acts chapter 4, because this is where things really became dynamite. They *were filled again*—why? Because they craved something. What was it? They desired boldness for their great commission.

> *"...grant to Your servants that with all boldness they may speak Your word, by stretching out Your hand to heal, and that signs and wonders may be done through the name of Your holy Servant Jesus." And when they had prayed, the place where they were assembled together was shaken; and they were all filled with the Holy Spirit, and they spoke the word of God with boldness... And with great power the apostles gave witness to the resurrection of the Lord Jesus. And great grace was upon them all* (Acts 4:29-31,33).

Boldness in Old Testament Greek means "might, power, strength, strong."[2] In the New Testament Greek, it means "free and fearless confidence, cheerful courage, and assurance."[3] It describes the confidence with which Christians can approach God because of the redeeming work of Christ.[4]

The transliterated word for miracle in Greek is *dunamis*.[5] It means strength, ability, and power for performing miracles. It's God's dynamite power. We see *dunamis* used all through the New Testament in the context of this power: 120 times in the King James Version—seven times for *miracle*, four times for *might*, seven times for *strength*, 77 times for *power*, and eleven times for *mighty work*. Do you see the connection between the words "boldness," and "miracle"? Might, mighty, power, strength, strong. They prayed for boldness— they prayed for miracles. They prayed for God's dynamite power *in* them and *through* them, which would manifest in mighty works—in miracles, hallelujah.[6]

Boldness for what? They asked for boldness to go and preach the Gospel to strangers in far off lands because of their confident assurance that, by the holy name of the Father's Son, signs and wonders would be done. The disciples already operated in the power of God, but they had revelation of the need for evangelism, and they effectively said, "We can't do it without more power. We know there's another dimension. We need that dimension of power to do Your will." They needed the fullness of God now.

The Holy Spirit filled believer after believer after believer, even after the day of Pentecost. Paul's epistles and the Book of Acts show repeated and continual empowerment as well as the impartation of powerful and awesome gifts for ministry.

CONTINUOUS POWER = CONTINUOUS FILLING

Every believer has the Holy Spirit; however, Scripture is clear that we're to be continually filled (see Rom. 8:9,16; Eph. 5:18). While the baptism of the Holy Spirit is the specific event that introduces us to the ongoing process of living a Spirit-empowered life, we're to have a constant hunger for God, seeking to be filled, filled, and filled again with His power.

You see, there's a difference between being full and being filled with the Holy Spirit. God gave us the Holy Spirit in His fullness, but we need to seek constant filling of Him over and above the initial indwelling and subsequent baptism of the Holy Spirit. We need the abiding presence of the Holy Spirit—the infilling fullness of the habitation of God in our lives. The key to the disciples' power was in continuous filling—being filled and filled and filled again. They were filled in Acts 2, filled twice in Acts 4 (see Acts 4:8,31), and filled again in Acts 7.

We know that Stephen was full of the Holy Spirit, because the Bible says "they chose Stephen, a man *full* of faith and the *Holy Spirit*" (Acts 6:5). Stephen, full of "faith and power," already filled with the Holy Spirit, did great wonders, signs, and miracles among the people (see Acts 6:8). As they stoned him, he had a vision of Jesus, and the Bible says, "he, *being full* (present tense) of the Holy Spirit..." (see Acts 7:55). Stephen was full and stayed that way because it was a constant filling that kept him full. Paul says, "And do not be drunk with wine, in which is dissipation; but *be filled* with the Spirit" (Ephesians 5:18). *Be filled* infers an action that is ongoing.

What does "being filled" look like? When my team and I were in Nigeria, Africa, the Lord gave me revelation of this every morning, and every morning God came down and filled me with the lightnings of God. Every morning I had a fresh filling, and I was filled and became full with the power of God.

Being filled with the Spirit is a command. It is a present continuous action. The Church was filled on the day of Pentecost (see Acts 2:4). Peter and John were filled again, the deacons were filled again, Steven was filled again, the apostles Paul and Barnabas were filled continuously, and other disciples were filled with joy and the Holy Spirit (see Acts 4:8,13; 6:13; 7:55; 9:17; 11:24; 13:52).

Do you want zest, zeal, gusto, passion, enthusiasm, and a spiritual appetite? Do you want to burn with passion for God? Dig deep into Him! Do you wonder why the lives of others with less talent or fewer gifts than you seem much fuller and livelier? Passion motivates and moves them. In those people, sin is less frequent too. The key is that they are constantly filled with the Spirit and thus live a dynamic Christian life, their hunger constantly attended to.

The key to being full of the power of God is to be full of the Holy Spirit. Speaking in tongues doesn't make you full of Him. Being full takes being filled, filled, and filled again. This comes about by the anointing—by allowing the Kingdom of Heaven to fill and possess you! There is one thing I discovered that I must share with you here. As full as I can be at times, I can be just as empty the next day. It's not that the Holy Spirit has left me, but I've gone off course—I've changed dynamics. When I hang around Heaven and the Holy Spirit, it's a constant replenishment, but when I don't, the fuel tank gets to the "add fuel" level. Don't let your spiritual tank hover on empty; you desperately need refilling of high-octane Holy Spirit fuel. What does being filled and full look like? Fill yourself with the reality of the following:

- "Or do you not know that your body is the temple of the Holy Spirit who is in you, whom you have from God, and you are not your own? For you were bought at a price; therefore glorify God in your body and in your spirit, which are God's" (1 Cor. 6:19-20).

- Jesus, "*being filled* with the Holy Spirit," was led into the wilderness by the Spirit so that He could resist the greatest temptations known to man (see Luke 4:1).

- The baby Elizabeth carried leapt in her womb, and *she was filled* with the Holy Spirit and loudly (boldly) prophesied to Mary, "Blessed are you among women, and blessed is the fruit of your womb" (Luke 1:42).

- The Holy Spirit *filled* Zechariah powerfully to prophesy (see Luke 1:67).

- John the Baptist, Luke 1:15 tells us, would be *filled* with the Holy Spirit, even from his mother's womb. Note what Jesus said about him—that there had never been one greater than John the Baptist (see Matt. 11:11).

- In selecting the seven deacons, the disciples called for seven men "of good reputation" and *full of the Holy Spirit* and wisdom (see Acts 6:3).

- Barnabas was described as "a good man, *full of the Holy Spirit* and of faith. And a great many people were added to the Lord" (Acts 11:24).

- "The disciples were filled with joy and with the Holy Spirit" (Acts 13:52).

We see through these examples much power. Power to resist temptation, to discern, to prophesy, to witness, and to have knowledge, wisdom, revelation, good reputation, faith, and *joy*.

HUNGER COMES BY REASON OF USE

Every believer, whether spiritually mature or not, should hunger after the Lord. There are those who are satisfied, and that is sad, because they think that there's only a certain measure of spiritual fatness for them, so they guard it for themselves. There are those who are so fat they can't move. All they do is go from conference to conference, but there's no room for fresh oil, and the oil inside turns rancid from lack of use. Then there are those like Paul who hunger for the constant filling because they empty themselves constantly so that they can be filled. Hunger translates as wanting more and more of God—continuously. You won't hunger if you don't pour Him out into the lives of the lost or the sick. You get hungry by reason of "use," walking in the anointing, using up the fuel so that He can replenish you with more of Himself.

I want you to do something. Try this: don't leave your bedroom in the morning without seeking Him. Spend time in His presence to receive the high-octane fuel of the Holy Spirit before you do anything else. I just lie on my carpet until I bring Heaven into my room, until I feel the fire of God fill my body from top to bottom.

Then, ask God to show you where to use that fuel in your day, and watch it spill over into everything. The fuel of the Holy Spirit will take care of any doubt you may have of His presence in your life, of His power, and of His ability and willingness to work and move through you. That boldness will give you the assurance that God is everything He says He is—and much more. The Holy Spirit will bring life to the *Word* and fill your words with power to boost your faith, your boldness, and your confidence.

CONFIDENCE, ASSUREDNESS

John the Baptist sent his disciples to Jesus to ask if He was the Coming One, most likely not for his own sake, but for the sake of his disciples. Jesus wanted to assure them that He is the Messiah:

Now it came to pass, when Jesus finished commanding His twelve disciples, that He departed from there to teach and to preach in their cities. And when John had heard in prison about the works of Christ, he sent two of his disciples and said to Him, "Are You the Coming One, or do we look for another?" Jesus answered and said to them, "Go and tell John the things which you hear and see: The blind see and the lame walk; the lepers are cleansed and the deaf hear; the dead are raised up and the poor have the gospel preached to them. And blessed is he who is not offended because of Me" (Matthew 11:1-6).

Essentially the questions were, "Has Jesus come, or hasn't He come? Is He alive, is He for me?" Today our question might be, "Are you the religion I need to know? How do I know if it is sound? How do I know this isn't a cult in disguise? How do I know that I have the right God out of all the millions of gods?"

However, Jesus didn't have to preach anything more to them to convince them. He said, (my paraphrase) "Just look at what you've seen, at what I've done, and you will know! Don't look at My preaching, My teaching, or My theology! The blind see, the lame walk, the lepers are cleansed, the deaf hear, the dead are raised up, and the poor aren't exempted from it all. Is this not validation enough?"

Christ was saying, essentially, "You've missed the manifestation of *Me*, the One whom the Word is about. Never mind what I've preached! Go tell them about what I do, tell them about My works, and in so doing, you'll have preached the Gospel!"

Paul understood what that meant. He made it his goal and aim to preach Christ where the name of Christ had never been uttered. He had a heart for souls and was excited about tearing down the walls that separated Christianity from the lost and dying world. More than anything else, he loved being an apostle of Christ, going out into the world to save the lost and the captive with the power of the Gospel!

Go Into the World

We are so consumed in the Church today with "in-house" vision that we forget about going where the name of Christ has never been named. Churches have conferences for whom? Believers. Ministries have conferences for whom? Believers. What about going into the world? Many of the conferences of today are what I term "righteous" conferences, where everything is about doing things right and learning in-house, rather than fueling at the feet of Jesus and then going out into the world with the power of the Gospel as our learning and application tool. There are conferences all over the place and all the time. Prophetic ones, worship ones, impartation ones, spiritual warfare ones, and the list goes on. But I say, "What if?" What if, for every conference, we hold a crusade? What if, for every 5,000 conference invitations we send out to believers, we send out 10,000 mailers that go to the houses of the unsaved, telling them about Jesus?

What if? What if we advertise our conferences on secular radio and television and in secular newspapers and other forms of media? Do you know that some pastors bring me into their city and just want to keep me within their church's four walls? They don't even invite other churches to come or advertise outside of their church into the world. They want me to pour into their church, and theirs only. How sad! I'll ask, "What have you done to prepare for my coming and to see miracles?" And I'll find out they sent maybe 500 invitations to their church membership.

How are we ever going to take our cities for Christ if all we do in the Church today is try to fatten ourselves up without taking the oil and letting it rub off of us or flow through us to the world? We have to have bigger goals and be like Paul, making it our aim and goal to go where the name of Christ has never been named, because that is where the Gospel will *fully be able to function and operate in the power that the Gospel is.*

For one particular conference of mine several years ago in Canada, I spent thousands of dollars advertising on secular radio, television, and in newspapers. Guess what happened? Two hundred East Indian souls came to the conference, and many went home saved, healed, and delivered. This never would have happened had I not let the unsaved know about the conference. Also, during our breaks, our team went out into the streets and marketplace, and 50 more were added to our number.

I understand the need for growing family in the Body of Christ, and I understand why we hold potlucks, seminars, retreats, or meetings in or through our churches, and it's all good. However, do those things keep us too busy to go out into the world with the good news of the Gospel? Do they equip us for evangelism? Today churches seem generally more focused on keeping the congregation happy, rather than on acting as an equipping and fueling center where they can fill up with the Holy Spirit, as the early church did, and then go out into the world and evangelize the Jerusalems, the Samarias, and the Judeas, and then take it to the outer most parts. But something's happened throughout time; religiosity has infiltrated so many churches, along with the rules and traditions of men that have somewhat diluted our purpose.

WHERE'S THE EVANGELISTIC FERVOR?

I want to see the release of evangelistic fervor come into the hearts of God's people, to stir us to take mighty demonstrations of the Spirit of God into the malls, the streets, the ghettos, the hospitals, and the teen hangouts. It's our commission, and it's the ministry of Jesus. When Jesus called His 12 disciples, He gave them power to do the work—power over unclean spirits, to cast them out, and power to heal all kinds of sickness and diseases (see Matt. 10:1). He not only gave them power, He gave you power, and He gave your children power. Consider that the power went first to the 12. Then it saw exponential increase and leapt to 70, then to 120, then to 3,000, and then it went to as many as the Lord our God will call: "For the promise is to you and to your children, and to all who are afar off, as many as the Lord our God will call" (Acts 2:39).

Do you know that no matter what office you have in the Body of Christ, be it apostle, evangelist, or any of the other five-fold ministry offices, you are first and foremost a disciple? He gave power to His disciples—you're His disciple. You are a disciple of Jesus. Say it aloud, right now, and let it sink in. "I, Todd Bentley, am a disciple of Jesus." Yes I am, and yes you are! He promised us the Holy Spirit. His promise *is* the Holy Spirit. The promise releases us into "many wonders and signs" (see Acts 2:43).

POWER AS YOU GO

When He said, "This promise is for you" He was actually talking about the promise of the Holy Spirit. The promise of the Holy Spirit was for us. And what does that promise do for us? It releases us into the impossible. "…and many wonders and signs were done through the apostles" (Acts 2:43). That promise is for you, your children, and as many as the Lord our God will call, so that when the Holy Spirit comes upon you, you can be a witness not in word only but in power.

Jesus promised us power as "we go." Recall that He told the disciples, "As you go, preach, saying, 'The kingdom of heaven is at hand'" (Matt. 10:7). All in one breath, He continued that instruction: "Heal the sick, cleanse the lepers, raise the dead, cast out demons. Freely you have received, freely give" (Matt. 10:8).

Why is it, though, that we have many people preaching God's Word today and not nearly enough demonstrating the power of the Word, as Christ told us to? Heaven is as open to us as believers today as it was for Christ 2,000 years ago. God wants you to preach the fullness of salvation with demonstration of it by the power of the Holy Spirit. It's called "doing the stuff." Listen, who lives in you? The Holy Spirit. Who raised Jesus from the dead? The Spirit of God. Who gives life to our mortal body? The Spirit of God who dwells in us (see Rom. 8:11). Of course we can preach the Gospel of power. Of course signs, wonders, and miracles will follow us (see Mark 16:17). Of course we'll carry Heaven with us. Of course!

JUST DO THE STUFF

Preachers and teachers abound—there are many messengers, but we have to stop separating healing and deliverance, signs and wonders, from the Gospel. We have to stop slotting them into different categories. Yes, there are specific gifts and functions in the Body, but we are all called to heal the sick and cleanse the leper, cast out demons, and raise the dead. We all have the same Holy Spirit, don't we? We're all disciples, aren't we? You don't have to have a deliverance ministry to cast out a demon. You don't have to have a healing ministry to pray for a lame leg. You don't have to hold the office of teacher to teach. Those offices have a great place, but you are called, as we all are, to do the stuff that Jesus did. We have the priestly authority to do so.

The Kingdom of God is not a kingdom in word only, but also in power (see 1 Cor. 4:20). It doesn't matter how much you know theologically about the process of salvation or healing—it does matter, though, what you *do* with that knowledge, because knowledge for the sake of knowledge is dead, lifeless, useless. Applied knowledge is a treasure. You have the knowledge; God wants you to apply it. Lay hands on someone, cast out a devil, pray for someone on his or her deathbed. What's the worst that can happen? Listen, Jesus spoke to His disciples—He speaks to us.

Note in Matthew 10:8 that raising the dead came *before* casting out devils. This speaks of power, friends—the great and wonderful power of God that says if you are casting out devils you can do everything else. If you can preach the Gospel, you can heal the sick. If you can heal the sick, you can preach the Gospel. If you can preach the Gospel, you can cleanse the leper. If you can cleanse the leper, you can preach the Gospel. If you can heal the sick, you can raise the dead. If you can raise the dead, you can cast out demons. If you can cast out demons, you can preach the Gospel. If you can heal the sick, you can cleanse the leper. If can cleanse the leper, you can raise the dead. If you can raise the dead, you can preach the Gospel. If you can preach the Gospel, you can heal the sick. It's all the same thing! It doesn't get any harder. It's all about Him. It's the Kingdom. It's the Gospel. It's the message, and the Holy Spirit brings a demonstration of the power of God.

How hungry are you? Come on, how hungry are you to know God and His power and to come into a release of that power that will fill you continuously and bring you into a new level of faith and power? Stephen was full of faith and power right until his end, but do you know why he was full? Because he was full of the Holy Spirit, and that's all you need. You don't have to try to get more faith and power, just get full of the precious Holy Spirit.

As we've learned now, the ministry of the Kingdom of God brings creative power out of the heavens to override the natural and the impossible here, and it releases the supernatural power of God. With the heavens accessible to us, we are able to see, taste, hear, and know what the Father is doing, and we can confidently witness with the same power that Jesus did, because we set our minds and hearts in Heaven too. Jesus opened it up for all believers to lay hands on the sick, cast out devils, and raise the dead, because we have the same anointing of the Holy Spirit that He had.

We cannot force God's hand by our actions, our theology, our protocols, or anything else. He moves because He wants to, because He loves us, because He is our Father and He loves us so much that He sent us Jesus to bear the weight that we cannot. He doesn't move in power or act because we have a secret formula whereby we can force Him, nor does He move because of our own merits. He moves because of *who* He is.

We've learned why miracles must happen in the presence of the Holy Spirit and the powerful Gospel of Jesus Christ. I hope that you've studied and meditated on the powerful Scriptures and teachings found in this chapter so that you, too, will become excited, bold, and confident in your faith and go out into the world, "to whom He was not announced," that they "shall see; and those who have not heard shall understand" (Rom. 15:21).

Ask the Holy Spirit to reveal to you how He wants you to apply what you've learned in this chapter as you take the Gospel of the Kingdom to the world so that you can become more like Jesus, in heart, mind, and deed as you witness and demonstrate the power of God.

If you know you believe and have faith but have found it difficult to step out and share the message of the God's Kingdom, repent and take active steps of faith based on His promises found in Matthew 10.

Confidence Builder for Power Evangelism (Acts 4:31)

It's vital to have confidence in the Gospel and God in us to:

- Be bold for Him

- Be Excited

- Rid ourselves of apathy

- Become passionate

- Thrust!

- Spontaneously preach

- Press in

Commission to Power Evangelism (Matthew 10)

As you go:

- He gives you *power* (verse 1).

- He'll *confirm* your *word* (verse 7).

- Preach the "Kingdom of Heaven is at hand."

- Preach the Gospel *and* heal the sick (verse 8).

- What to do if you're rejected (verse 14).

- God will give you what to speak (verse 18).

- God speaks through you (verse 20).

- They'll hate you, but that's OK (verse 22)!

- Be bold, shout it from the rooftops (verse 27).

- They can't kill the soul (verse 28). (See Acts 14:22.)

- He is with you (verses 29-30)!

- If you can preach the Gospel, you can heal, deliver, cast out demons, raise the dead—you can do all things because there's power in the Word.

⟳ PERSONAL PRAYER

Thank You, Jesus, that You healed everyone and that You are still the same today. Let the seed of what I've learned here today grow into a radical faith, that You would help me to obey that same commission You gave to Your disciples to heal the sick, cleanse the lepers, raise the dead, and cast out demons. Oh Lord, give me a greater realization and revelation of You with me—the message of the Cross; make Your power a reality to me. Destroy every lie the enemy has sown in me to prevent me from sharing Your awesome power and beauty and the message of the Kingdom with others. Forgive me for unbelief in Your healing, miracle-working power. Root out all unbelief and fear, apathy, and complacency and help me to step out in radical faith and faith in Your Kingdom power. I pray that the Gospel of the Kingdom becomes Your word of life for the lost, the captive, the oppressed, the sick, and the prisoner. Put feet to my faith, Lord, as I step out into the world. Make me like Jesus, the One who destroys the works of the devil and brings freedom and healing to the lives of people everywhere. I want to preach and demonstrate Your full Gospel, the incredible good news of the Kingdom. Let Your Kingdom be manifest through my life today. You're awesome, God! In Jesus' name, I pray, amen.

ENDNOTES

1. See Romans 15:19. See also *Spirit of God* in Matthew 3:16; 12:28; John 4:24 (God is Spirit); Acts 2:17; Romans 8:14; 1 Corinthians 2:14; 3:16; 6:11; 7:40; 12:3; 2 Corinthians 3:3; 4:30; Philemon 3:3; 1 Peter 4:14; 1 John 4:2. Some Old Testament references: Genesis 1:2; 41:38; Exodus 31:3; 35:31; Numbers 24:2; 1 Samuel 10:10; 11:6; 19:20; 19:23; 2 Chronicles 15:1; 24:20; Job 33:4; Isaiah 61:11; Daniel 5:14.

2. Brown, Driver, Briggs, and Gesenius, *The Old Testament Hebrew Lexicon*, s.v. "Oz," (Strong's Hebrew #5797), http://www.studylight.org/lex/heb/view.cgi?number=5797 (accessed 10 November 2007).

3. Thayer and Smith, *The New Testament Greek Lexicon*, s.v. "Parrhesia," http://www.studylight.org/lex/grk/view.cgi?number=3954 (accessed 10 November 2007).

4. See 2 Corinthians 3:4-6,12; Hebrews 10:19; 1 John 2:28; 4:17; Trent C. Butler, ed., *Holman Bible Dictionary* (1991), s.v. "Boldness," http://www.studylight.org/dic/hbd/view.cgi?number=T998 (accessed 25 June 2008).

5. Strong's Exhaustive Concordance of the Bible, s.v. "Dunamis," (Greek #1411).

6. Study dunamis power/miracles in Acts: 1:8; 2:22; 3:12; 4:7; 4:33; 6:8; 8:10; 8:13; 10:38; 19:11 (KJV).

KINGDOM INVASION

The Kingdom of God is indestructible, constantly increasing, and everlasting. It advances, it fills, and it fulfills. While every other kingdom will someday shatter, God's Kingdom cannot be shaken and will never be destroyed.

> *In the days of these kings the God of Heaven will set up a Kingdom which shall never be destroyed; and the Kingdom shall not be left to other people; it shall break in pieces and consume all these kingdoms, and it shall stand forever* (Daniel 2:44).

It advances, advances, advances! As it advances, it consumes and then fills everything with itself—with the very presence and glory of God. It advances, overtakes, and recovers all. It cannot be shaken.

> *Therefore, since we are receiving a kingdom which cannot be shaken, let us have grace, by which we may*

serve God acceptably with reverence and godly fear. For our God is a consuming fire (Hebrews 12:28-29).

To synchronize Heaven and earth, we need to have a revelation, a clear Kingdom mindset, about the ever-increasing vastness of the Kingdom of God and of the glory that is to fill it. We can't let our Kingdom mindset be puny; it's infinite and enormous. Let's enlarge our outlook!

Daniel, the prophet, in the interpretation God gave him of King Nebuchadnezzar's dream, prophesied of a coming Kingdom that would fill the earth, overtaking every other kingdom. The king had seen a "rock cut out of a mountain but not by human hands" that would become a great mountain and *fill* the earth (see Dan. 2:20-21). This rock was metaphorically the Messiah, the Rock, none other than our Lord Jesus Christ, who would establish and rule the Kingdom of righteousness with the saints through His death and resurrection, enforcing and filling the earth with God's righteousness, peace, and mercy (see Deut. 32:4). Daniel later saw, in a parallel dream and visions of his own, the Son of Man to whom was given "authority, glory, and sovereign power," and "all peoples, nations and men of every language worshipped Him" (see Dan. 7:13-14 NIV).

The filling of the earth is consistent with a promise given to the Israelites while in the wilderness between Egypt and the promised land of Israel. After one particular time of rebellion against God, Moses asked God to forgive them, and God replied, "I have pardoned, according to your word; but truly, as I live, all the earth shall be filled with the glory of the Lord" (Num. 14:20-21). That's

His promise, that He would *fill* the earth with His glory. This should be the central hope of every believer. Jesus said, "The Kingdom of God is at hand." The Kingdom has come to fill and invade our lives. It's a powerful blueprint for living.

Do Business Until He Comes

Jesus told us to "do business till I come" (Luke 19:13b). The Kingdom of God is a strategy for taking ground for the glory of the Lord to fill. Do you want to take the land for the glory of God? The Kingdom of God is our guide and framework for filling the earth with His glory. "Here it is," says Jesus, "the Kingdom of God is within your reach. I've taken care of everything." Grab it, lay hold of it, receive it, and base your life on this awesome opportunity to live a naturally supernatural life under the divine rule and reign of the King of kings—Jesus, the King of Glory. He calls each one of us to move into this new reality. Jesus' call to repentance was a call to change your purpose, to about-face, to change your mind, for God's Kingdom is here, available to you now, not only in the future (see Matt. 4:17).

Kingdom Facets

There are two facets to this Kingdom growth and filling: the aspects we can see in the natural, such as the increase in numbers of the Body of Christ (the Church), and the spiritual side, the growth of the Kingdom of God in the hearts of those who recognize and serve the King of the Kingdom.

Ever since the time of Adam and Eve, the Kingdom has grown and advanced as people throughout the ages have resolved to take ground for the Kingdom. Of believers today, the Bible says that from the days of John the Baptist until now the Kingdom of Heaven suffers violence and the violent take it by force (see Matt. 11:12). Why by force?

Every single person who enters into the Kingdom must press in to grow and advance the Kingdom because our flesh resists the Kingdom. Jesus explained this beautifully in the Parable of the Sower, showing that the good news of the Kingdom (the seed) grows in our hearts but that some hearts are too hard and thus don't hear and retain it (see Matt. 13:3-8,18-23). Other hearts aren't deep enough to overcome opposition, and the seed of His word dies. Some people let His word grow, but the things of the world choke it so that the person's life does not bear fruit. The Kingdom grows when the person receives the seed into good soil (the heart) and chooses to let it produce.

Of the Kingdom, Jesus said in another parable that it is like a man who scatters seeds on the soil and the seeds produce on their own:

> *And He said, "The kingdom of God is as if a man should scatter seed on the ground, and should sleep by night and rise by day, and the seed should sprout and grow, he himself does not know how. For the earth yields crops by itself: first the blade, then the head, after that the full grain in the head. But when the grain ripens, immediately he puts in the sickle, because the harvest has come"* (Mark 4:26-29).

KINGDOM PARABLES

The Kingdom Parables in Matthew 13 reveal much about the Kingdom of God and its visible and invisible growth and workings in our lives and in the Church. All of these parables indicate to the hearers that Jesus is inviting us to enter into something immediately accessible.

Jesus taught these parables to the multitudes and crowds from a boat, which He often used as His "pulpit." Imagine Jesus for a moment in the center of that beautiful backdrop of what would be a seemingly endless expanse of sea that met an endless breadth of sky, and then picture the endlessness of the Kingdom of God with Christ reigning in it.

People have often said of parables that they are earthly stories with heavenly meaning or significance. Is it any wonder, therefore, that Jesus often spoke of the Kingdom of Heaven in this manner?

In the Parable of the Mustard Seed, Jesus compared an aspect of the Kingdom to a mustard seed that a man planted in his field. He taught that however unimpressive the Kingdom of God might look to us now, it's growing into something tremendously big—from a tiny mustard seed to a bush large enough to provide shelter to us (see Mark 4:30-32).

He also compared the Kingdom to yeast—a woman hid yeast in flour until it spread throughout the dough. A little leaven will leaven the whole lump. A stone becomes a mountain that fills the whole earth. Do you see the nature of growth? The Kingdom has grown and is growing and will grow, filling and transforming our hearts and the world.

Why? Why would Jesus go to such great lengths to explain these Kingdom principles to us?

First, we are the treasure He has found. In the Parable of the Hidden Treasure, Jesus explained that the Kingdom of Heaven is like a treasure that a man finds and then hides in a field. He sells all he has and buys the entire field because of the treasure he himself hid there. The field is the world, and the man is Jesus who gave all that He had to buy the field for the treasure. What treasure could be so wonderful that Jesus would give His life to purchase it? Us! We are that treasure He rejoices over.

What kind of treasure are we? We are the pearl of great price. Jesus told the story about the merchant seeking beautiful pearls who, when he had found one pearl of great price, went and sold all that he had and bought it. The buyer in this story is Jesus, and we are the pearl that He sees as so valuable that He would gladly give all to have us forever.

Second, Jesus wanted to ensure that the disciples understood the things of the Kingdom of which He spoke, and so He also explained that the Kingdom of Heaven is like a "householder who brings out of his treasure things new and old" (Matt. 13:52). Everyone who really knows and treasures God's Word will know the old and learn the new of the Kingdom!

INCREASE OF HIS GOVERNMENT AND PEACE

The nature of the Kingdom of God is "of the increase of His government and peace there will be no end" (Isa. 9:7). Just as the rock would become a great mountain and fill the earth, just as a mustard seed grows and overtakes, just as a little leaven leavens the whole lump, so the nature of the Kingdom of God is that it grows, it fills, and it invades. The Bible shouts out and declares, "The earth will be filled with the knowledge of the glory of the Lord, as the waters cover the sea" (Hab. 2:14). Today, we're awaiting that sovereign day in which God will pour out His glory; however, God also says, "Arise, shine; for your light has come! And the glory of the Lord *is risen* upon you" (Isa. 60:1). This is no earthly light but light that emanates and shines from the glory of the Lord. It's the light of Jesus in the Transfiguration when "His face shone like the sun, and His clothes became as white as the light" (Matt. 17:2).

The King of the Kingdom, God Himself, allowed Himself to be born on earth as a human being (see Luke 1:30-33). Thus, when God came to earth as a Man, His Kingdom came to the earth and followed Him wherever He went. The enemies of the Kingdom couldn't stand His presence, and though they killed Him, death couldn't even stand before Him. God came to bring His Kingdom to earth, to bring His Kingdom near to man, and He did it through Jesus. The Kingdom grew as people obeyed His call to follow Him, as people sought Him out, heard, and believed His words. It was during the time of Jesus and through Him and through those who followed and believed in Him that the Kingdom was made visible to the world. People "saw" the Kingdom through the good news Jesus preached and taught, and through the sudden disappearance of the consequences of sin—sickness and demonic oppression—which Jesus and His disciples healed and cast out. Sin and sickness could not be in the presence of the King or in His Kingdom. They are contrary to the laws of the Kingdom. Shortage and lack couldn't even stand in His Presence, nor could our sinful nature—everything was subject to the King.

THE PROMISE OF THE COMFORTER AND HELPER

Jesus gave His disciples all of the keys to the Kingdom of God during His short time on the earth. Before physically leaving and sending them out into the world, He promised them that the Comforter, the Holy Spirit, would come and live in them, would guide them in truth, and would show them more of Himself (see John 14:16-19). After Jesus ascended into Heaven, just as He promised, the Holy Spirit came. The Holy Spirit didn't just fall upon the 11 disciples first. He alighted upon 120 of them, and by the end of that day, 3,000 more. Hallelujah!

Jesus sent us the Holy Spirit so that He could live within us, so that the Kingdom of God and the glory and presence of the King would permeate, infiltrate, fill, transform, and advance not only in our own lives, but also in the lives of the multitudes all over the earth, for the end-time glory and purpose.

For 33 years, the Kingdom of God was present in a single human body, that of Jesus the King. Because of His death and resurrection, the Kingdom became present and a reality in thousands of bodies! These who were now subjects of the King would act, advance, fill, and move with His full authority. But although the King and His Kingdom were in many bodies, they were truly one Body, because Jesus prayed for believers, that they would be set apart and made one with Himself, the Father, and each other in perfect unity so that the world may believe. Jesus gave us the glory that the Father gave the Son. We were made perfect in One. Jesus also prayed to the Father that we would be with Him always. Read this, it's powerful:

> *I do not pray for these alone, but also for those who will believe in Me through their word; that they all may be one, as You, Father, are in Me, and I in You; that they also may be one in Us, that the world may believe that You sent Me. And the glory which You gave Me I have given them, that they may be one just as We are One: I in them, and You in Me; that they may be made perfect in one, and that the world may know that You have sent Me, and have loved them as You have loved Me. Father, I desire that they also whom You gave Me may be with Me where I am, that they may behold My glory which You have given Me; for You loved Me before the foundation of the world. O righteous Father! The world has not known You, but I have known You; and these have known that You sent Me. And I have declared to them Your name, and will declare it, that the love with which You loved Me may be in them, and I in them"* (John 17:20-26).

All of us who believe are the Body of Christ on earth—one in the Spirit. As such, we are brothers and sisters in Christ, citizens of the Father's Kingdom, and carriers of the Kingdom within, carriers of the King, carriers of His glory and presence into a dark world. Everywhere we go we have the potential to carry Heaven with us, opening Heaven's portals all over the world as His ambassadors.

When Jesus said that the Kingdom of Heaven is at hand, He meant it—the Kingdom of God is within us, and available to us 24/7. It is without end, as God is without end. It is as big as God is—unfathomably big! The more time you spend in His presence, the more His glory fills your space. In the presence of His glory, your destiny unfolds, miracles and healings happen, and demons flee.

The Lord told a pastor acquaintance of mine from Las Vegas who had attended one of our Open Heaven Conferences in Abbotsford, British Columbia, Canada, to buy a two-person tent to use as a makeshift "tent of meeting." It would be his secret place to meet with God. He set it up in his living room, and placed a Bible inside, and every day he'd enter in and worship God. He called one day and said, "Todd, I'm filling up my tent with the glory of God. And when it's full, I'm going to fill my house with the glory. When that's full, I'm going to fill my city block up with it, then my city, my region, and the nation!"

That's the nature of the Kingdom of God: it grows, increases, and fills. This story shows how important it is that we are all "carriers" of the Kingdom, that God's presence is so overflowing in our lives that it spills out everywhere, touching people around us. It's what I like to term, "Kingdom radius." How much of the Kingdom is spilling out of you and how far-reaching is it?

KINGDOM SPHERES AND RADIUSES

The Kingdom can fill every space in our radius or sphere of influence. The apostle Peter had a six- or seven-foot Kingdom radius that was as close as his shadow. The Kingdom of God was at hand in that everywhere Peter passed by, people clamored to have even his shadow fall on them or upon their sick loved ones (see Acts 5:15). Now think about that for a moment. Wherever Peter went, he brought Heaven to earth within that six- or seven-foot sphere. Peter was a living, breathing manifestation of the Kingdom, and wherever he went, he brought Heaven down to earth—the Kingdom touched people.

When God's Kingdom manifests, the devil looses his hold on lives. That's what happened when Brian, a worship leader, and some friends, musicians, and dancers visited a mall in Redding, California, to worship. When the worship leader and entourage took a break, just as they sat down, a man walked by the area where they'd just worshiped. The man took some drugs out of his pocket, threw them on the ground, and kept walking. Why do you think this happened? A heavenly portal had opened, and the man encountered "Heaven now." Since drugs don't exist in Heaven, the enemy lost his grip in that atmosphere of Heaven. That's the kingdom of Heaven in action!

Such is the Kingdom of God that it can fill every square inch or mile that you tread. The Bible declares that the earth will be filled with the knowledge of the glory of the Lord, as the waters cover the sea (see Hab. 2:14). Remember, the stone became a mountain, and the mountain filled the whole earth (see Dan. 2:34-35). The seed became a tree (see Matt. 13:31-32). The glory of the Lord in you can change the spiritual climate or atmosphere anywhere you go for massive revival.

We are responsible for filling the earth—filling cities, filling regions, and filling nations—with the Kingdom of God. God has said that when the Gospel of the Kingdom is preached to all nations, then the end will come (see Matt. 24:14). But what if God is waiting for us to partner with Him in the expansion of His Kingdom? Many of us have been waiting for the Rapture. We are waiting for the day in which God fulfills His promise and fills the whole earth with His glory. We are waiting for the sovereign day in which the end comes and Jesus returns; but Jesus is waiting for *you* to co-labor with Him to fill the earth with the knowledge of His glory.

The treasure of the Kingdom is hidden on earth in earthen vessels: you and me. We carry a treasure in these earthen vessels. It's a sovereign time to reveal this treasure and to share the Gospel. Yet here we are most of the time just waiting for that sovereign time or day when the end will come (see Matt. 24:14).

Arise and shine, for your light has come (see Isa. 60:1)! Do you know what God told Abraham? "Arise, walk in the land through its length and its width, for I give it to you" (Gen. 13:17). He showed Abraham the inheritance, and Abraham saw it and received it in his spirit. God also said to look and see the stars: "Look now toward heaven, and count the stars if you are able to number them. So shall your descendents be" (Gen. 15:5). He was saying, "Get it in your spirit Abraham! I want you to see your inheritance!"

Although I cover this more in the "Divine Inheritance" chapter, I want to emphasize now that God has given us dominion and authority to take ground for that inheritance. He said to Joshua, "Every place that the sole of your foot will tread upon I have give you, as I said to Moses (Josh. 1:3). He wants us to take ground, to take the land. We can't do that if we can't see what we're to take, nor if we don't know what we have, can we? We have to expand our Kingdom radius. How much of the Kingdom moves and manifests around you?

KINGDOM EMBASSY

I am a Canadian citizen, and my country has embassies all over the world. Embassies are a representation of your home country in another country. When I go to India, for instance, I can walk into the Canadian embassy there, and when I step on that piece of ground, effectively I am in Canada. I am in India, but I'm in Canada with all the rights, benefits, and protection that I enjoy in Canada. This is what the Kingdom of God on earth is like. We are ambassadors of the Kingdom of God. Everywhere we go, the Holy Spirit goes with us. It's like carrying a spiritual embassy around with you. We are in Heaven on earth with all the benefits and resources of Heaven available to us; with all the authority of Heaven backing us up.

Just as it is in the natural realm, I believe it's true of the spiritual realm—that God has set boundaries. When we travel through villages and towns, we often cross from one jurisdiction to another without even realizing it. Effectively, an invisible barrier separates one area of governmental control from another. Therefore, just as you might cross from one county to another naturally speaking, God has boundaries and property lines in the spirit. Think about the house you live in for a moment. If you own the house, then it's your property—you own it, and with ownership comes authority. It's your own small kingdom. Spiritually, what God has given you ownership of is the Kingdom for you. There the devil has no authority. When you are standing on your "property" in the spirit, then no plague, no sickness, no disease can harm you. Can you imagine taking cities and nations like that?

God demonstrated this principle powerfully to me when I was in Malawi, Africa. I had a "100-yard pitch" *given* to me by the government to hold a crusade. For the time of the mission, the area I preached in was mine. The government gave it to me, and ownership equals authority. In the stadium behind me, however, the government was having elections, and across the street from us was the local Muslim mosque, areas in which I had no authority.

HEAVEN'S SPIRITUAL DOORS AND PORTALS

I had my crusade ground for five days. I declared that, for the duration, this was the property of the Kingdom of God, this was "Heaven on earth." On one of the days, a boy who was deaf walked by the crusade. He didn't have any interest in the crusade, he was a Muslim who was on his way to the mosque, but as he walked by, his foot touched *my* field and his deaf ear popped open! There was another boy in the local hospital with an inoperable tumor on his leg. The doctors couldn't help him so they suggested that he go to the Todd Bentley crusade down the road. Someone even drove him onto the crusade grounds. The car door opened, and as soon as he set foot on the grass, the tumor fell away from his leg. Why? Because there are no tumors in Heaven, and Heaven was on my crusade grounds.

A man who was covered in literally hundreds of small tumors was sitting in a bar across town drinking beer. The owner of the bar decided to turn the radio on and tuned in to my crusade, which was being broadcast all across town. Because he was the owner of that piece of property, as soon as he made that choice, it was as if a portal had been opened for the power of God to come into the bar. The man with the tumors was instantly healed as, one after another, they fell from his body. He literally jumped into a taxicab and rushed down to the crusade to give his life to Jesus!

A local hospice had 65 terminally ill patients. A number of "ambassadors" from our team went into that place to represent Heaven and prayed for all 65 patients. Two days later, every single one of them had checked out of the hospital because God had healed them. An entire hospice emptied!

In the historic revival days of the past, of which I've read reports, some people even approaching city limits would be struck down by the power of God that filled the area. Men and women in the bars across town wouldn't even be able to get the beer mugs to their lips. That's what I want. I want to shine with the glory of the Lord so that wherever I go God's power will strike and transform people with His glory. "Arise and shine," saints, "for your light has come! And the glory of the Lord is risen upon you" (see Isa. 60:1).

SYNCHRONIZATION OF HEAVEN AND EARTH

The Kingdom of God increases and advances. God's Kingdom comes when Heaven and earth synchronize—when Heaven touches earth. His Kingdom comes when Heaven shows up in your world and your life plumbs with God's Kingdom. What do you know about Heaven? No disease, no sorrow, no pain, no poverty? As it is in Heaven, so may it be on earth! When Jesus said, "Pray...Your kingdom come" (Matt. 6:8-10), He was saying that things here aren't as they should be, that they aren't as they are in Heaven. When the Kingdom comes, everything that exists in Heaven invades earth. The

Kingdom of God is "as it is in Heaven" displayed on the earth. The Kingdom reflects on earth what Heaven is like *right now*.

Today on earth is not as it is in Heaven. It can be, however. That's why Jesus taught the disciples to pray for God's Kingdom to come. The Kingdom of God is the will of God being done or carried out on earth. He wants earth to become as it is in Heaven *now*. The enemy will do anything to oppose this wonderful divine plan. So pray for the Kingdom to come. Invite the atmosphere of Heaven into your life, your church, your city. Set a plumb line with Heaven and align your life with it.

Jesus said, "If you've seen Me you've seen the Father" (see John 14:9). Jesus healed every sickness and every disease among the people. That means that the healing of every sickness and every disease is the will of God, and the will of God is the Kingdom of God. But how can God's will be done on earth? Heaven is our model. We should not be seeking miracles, signs, and wonders in and of themselves, but for the increase of God's Kingdom. Miracles, signs, and wonders are an outflow of living in the reality of the supernatural, but if you are only pursuing the gift of healing, that is wrong. It's not wrong to desire to see people healed, but seeking God and His Kingdom first is a far greater thing (see Matt. 6:33).

PRESSING IN

We can't remain the same once we've responded to the call of Jesus to the Kingdom. Falling under the kingship and lordship of God is the use of all of our resources, talents, and abilities. Those who enter the Kingdom undergo radical and awesome change. We serve a Master who owns everything, and He owns our hearts (see Ps. 24:1). Does He own yours?

God calls us to press in to the Kingdom. How do we do this? We must be eager and earnest in going about our Kingdom business, seeking, searching, and receiving His words and treasuring His commands within us, always crying out for wisdom and understanding, discernment and knowledge. For the Lord gives us wisdom, which He tells us to seek after "as silver" and to search for as "hidden treasures" (see Prov. 2:1-4).

Then you will understand the fear of the Lord, and find the knowledge of God. For the Lord gives wisdom; from His mouth come knowledge and understanding; He stores up sound wisdom for the upright; He is a shield to those who walk uprightly; He guards the paths of justice, and preserves the way of His saints. Then you will understand righteousness and justice, equity and every good path (Proverbs 2:5-9).

DIVINE REVELATION AND COUNSEL

Revelation and counsel are important to welcoming and inviting the atmosphere of Heaven to invade earth. We carry the Kingdom of God with us, and we actually have the potential to open those portals of Heaven for the next believer passing through on Kingdom business.

The might of God operates by the counsel of God. The Spirit of might follows the Spirit of counsel. As we receive the counsel of

Heaven, we see a demonstration and manifestation of the might of Heaven here on earth. The prophet Isaiah cried out to God to rend the heavens, to come down so that the mountains would literally shake at His presence (see Isa. 64:1). Do you know how much might it takes to shake a mountain? Do you know that might is the Holy Spirit? Might is one of the seven aspects of the Holy Spirit, and might partners with counsel, just as the Spirit of wisdom and understanding, the Spirit of knowledge, and of the fear of the Lord partner (see Rev. 3:1; 4:5; 5:6; Isa. 11:2). Thus God says, "Not by might nor by power, but by My Spirit…Who are you, O great mountain? Before Zerubbabel you shall become a plain" (Zech. 4:6b,7a).

The work of rebuilding the temple was so huge and massive that it seemed like a great mountain. At this time in biblical history, some theologians believe that the great mountain may actually have been a mountainous pile of rubble at the temple site. God promises, however, that the rubble would be removed and the work carried on, not by your might, not by your power, but by His. He promised that by His Spirit, that great mountain would be leveled into a plain. Flat as a pancake! God actually warns us that those who take counsel not of Him and devise plans not of His Spirit add sin to sin (see Isa. 30:1).

As such, as we go about Kingdom business, we may face much rubble—mountains of rubble to break through. But we can change the spiritual atmospheres and climates by filling each place with the Kingdom and presence of the King, whether it's our home, our city, our place of work, or a specific region. We can ask God to rend the heavens, to open the floodgates of Heaven and rain revelation that will bring down our mountains and help us with our Kingdom endeavors. God will open Heaven for us and reveal to us our blueprints and strategy for His work. We can call down those unseen things that do not exist (as though they did) as we press toward the mark of our high calling as citizens and ambassadors of the Kingdom nation of Heaven (see Rom. 4:17b).

JESUS, THE ACCESS TO HEAVEN

In Jacob's revelatory dream of the ladder that we've already examined, there was now access to Heaven. He saw the angels of God ascending and descending. The angels ascended *from* the earth *and into Heaven and back* (see Gen. 28:12). Jesus said that "No one has ascended to Heaven but He who came down from Heaven, that is, the Son of Man who is in Heaven" (John 3:13). They ascended (from earth) into Heaven and descended back to earth with revelation, and back and forth they went. Jacob now knew that God was closer than ever and that there was real access and interaction between Heaven and earth. Jesus made it clear in John 1:51 that He Himself is the access to Heaven, the means by which Heaven comes down to us and by which we can go to Heaven.

In fact, Jesus invited John into Heaven. John describes seeing a door standing open in Heaven. Then He heard Jesus call in a voice as clear as a trumpet, "Come up here, and I will show you things which must take place after this" (Rev. 4:1b).

GEOGRAPHIC SPIRITUAL ATMOSPHERES

Notice also that Jacob dreamed from a specific place. He stopped at that desolate wilderness place that he afterward called Bethel (House of God) while on a journey to Syria to find a wife. Three times in one verse, *place* is mentioned: "He came to a *certain place,* and stayed there all night, because the sun had set. And he took one of the stones of *that place* and put it at his head, and he lay down in *that place* to sleep" (Gen. 28:11). Why the emphasis on a certain place? I believe it's because there was an open Heaven over that particular geographic place known as Bethel; for much earlier, before entering Canaan, Abraham, Jacob's grandfather, built an altar at Bethel, calling "on the name of the Lord," and he returned there after his time in Egypt (see Gen. 12:8; 13:3).

When Jacob returned with his large family, he again came to that place to hear the Lord's confirmation of the covenant, and this is where God changed his name to Israel. Again Jacob set up a stone monument (see Gen. 35:1-6; Hos. 12:4-5).[1]

Bethel became an important place, geographically and spiritually. It became a place of revelation. The Ark of the Covenant was kept there in the period of the judges (see Judg. 20:27). The tribes converged there upon Benjamin to avenge the moral atrocity at Gibeah (see Judg. 20:18-28). There they offered sacrifices to the Lord *seeking the Lord's direction* (see Judg. 21:1-4). It was there that Deborah and Samuel judged the civil and religious affairs of the Israelites in the area (see Judg. 4:5; 1 Sam. 7:16). Both of these prophets heard from God regularly.

Bethel became a target of attack by the enemy since archaeology shows that it was destroyed several times during this period. Other true prophets seem to have been attached to Bethel since Elijah encountered a group of them there as he traveled (see 2 Kings 2:2-3).

David considered the city significant enough to send it gifts during his flight as a fugitive from Saul (see 1 Sam. 30:27).

Before Jacob renamed that place, it had been called Luz, meaning "an almond tree." Do you know that an almond tree is one of the fastest budding and blossoming trees in the spring? It blossoms in January before other trees even break out. In Hebrew, the almond tree is called *Shakedh*, meaning "hasty tree."[2]

Interestingly, in the young prophet Jeremiah's first vision, he saw a branch of an almond tree. God commended him for being so observant. He said, "You have seen well, for I am ready to perform My word" (Jer. 1:12). In other words, "Jeremiah, you have seen a hasty tree which signifies that I will hasten My word, it will flourish and come to maturity to perform it!"[3]

Seeing well involves hearing from God and receiving the wise counsel of God. Might shows up to perform His word hastily—to make it grow, flourish, and mature. So that place where Jacob lay his head was significant and truly did have an open Heaven over it— there, God confirmed to Jacob the terms of the covenant that He'd given to both Abraham and to Isaac (see Gen. 12:1-3; 26:2-5; 28:3-4). Previously, Jacob had only been told by Isaac that the covenant was his. God was hastening His word, and He hastened it at that very place that his grandfather Abraham had called upon the Lord as he entered the Promised Land. Up until then, Jacob had only heard about this awesome and great God who had appeared to his forefathers, but now, here, this same God has a personal encounter with Jacob that would radically and hastily change and transform his life.

There are open Heavens over specific geographic places on earth today where the word of God hastens, flourishes, and matures. Have you ever heard the expression, "at the right place, at the right time?" Sometimes we are in areas where the spiritual heavens open on a grander scale for us. It may be a city, a region, a country, or a specific place God leads us to visit.

AREAS OF OPEN HEAVENS

In those areas are certain spiritual atmospheres that allow us to receive heightened revelation, or it's easier for us to spiritually ascend into the heavens and return to earth with revelation. Usually these open heavens came about by someone who had been there before us. Jacob's revelatory vision was one example of this, and I'm convinced that God sent him to this certain place for that reason.

Moravian Falls, North Carolina, is one of those places that I have visited, where some say the Moravians settled years ago after leaving Germany, where they had been a part of a 100-year prayer meeting. It is believed that they carried an open Heaven and saturated this area of America with prayer too, and interestingly, it is the place where Rick Joyner received revelation for his book, *The Final Quest.*

My first time in Moravian Falls, I could hardly sleep or shut off the revelation I received for three days and nights. When I did sleep, I'd have prophetic dreams. When I awoke, I'd have angelic visitations. Talk about feeling like a radio with big antennae! I received so much revelation that it was as though I kept tuning into different stations or broadcasts.

ATMOSPHERE

The atmosphere of a place has everything to do with revelation.

In Second Kings 3:15-17, the hand of the Lord came upon Elisha when the minstrel played. Elisha then received revelation and prophesied.

Worship and prayer establish God's throne on earth (see Ps. 22:3). The seraphim angels in Revelation 4:8 worship 24 hours a day every day. In an atmosphere of worship and prayer, we become transparent before God, and He gives us eyes to see into the spirit realm as Heaven opens. As we draw near to Him, God's glory presence becomes tangible, and the cherubim and seraphim—the creatures that cover and protect that glory—are activated.

Heaven invades earth when we pray, worship, and seek Him. These things rend the heavens, and God comes from Heaven with His wise counsel and mightily touches lives (see 2 Chron. 7:14). Where the minstrel plays and the people pray, the hand of the Lord comes.

We've just touched on the subject of open heavens and geographic prophetic atmospheres here, but you'll see it dotted throughout this book, because it is a vital key to Kingdom breakthrough. In my book, *The Reality of the Supernatural World,* I devote a whole chapter to it.

FOUNTAINS OF THE DEEP

Let me leave this with you in this chapter: when Heaven opens, two things happen at the same time. The fountains of the deep open, and the flood comes.

In the six hundredth year of Noah's life, in the second month, the seventeenth day of the month, on that day all the fountains of the great deep were broken up, and the windows of heaven were opened (Genesis 7:11).

See that? The fountains of the deep opened at the same time that Heaven opened, and then it rained (see Gen. 7:12). Although this story is about God's judgment and the waters are floodwaters, in a similar way, if we are in a wilderness and God wants to release rivers, springs, and pools of living water, the very fountains of the deep break open and spiritual waters flow through the wilderness. God even promises floods of blessing on our deserts: "For I will pour water on him who is thirsty, and floods on the dry ground; I will pour My Spirit on your descendants, and My blessing on your offspring" (Isa. 44:3).

Even in difficult times, the outpouring of His Spirit floods our lives, lifts us to a place of safety, and thrusts us into a new season of blessing. Would you like to receive a flood of the Holy Spirit? Rend the heavens. Desire deep fountains. When we drink of His waters, we will never thirst because the waters will become a fountain of water springing up into everlasting life (see John 4:14).

You may indeed travel into an area with an open well or an already open Heaven, but trust that you don't need to. You can dig new wells or rend the heavens again and again over every area because the water is plentiful enough for you to draw from your own deep fountain of revelation, for the floodgates of Heaven to rain blessings and revival upon you.

You can be the well in a dry land. You carry the glory in you. Dig deep, search deep. This might mean spending long hours in the Lord's presence. It might mean fasting and prayer, and seeing and practicing what Jesus Himself did, seeing what the Father is doing and doing so in a like manner (see John 5:19).

It's OK to ask God to take you into Heaven to show you what's going to happen next. When I ask that of Him, to show me what's going to happen next, I take the time to receive and fill my own well with revelation knowledge from the fountains of the deep.

In John 5:19, Jesus says, "I say to you, the Son can do nothing of Himself, but what He sees the Father do; for whatever He does, the Son also does in like manner." Here Jesus reveals to us the true key to Kingdom ministry: "I only do those things that I see the Father do." "My Father has been working," Jesus explains, "So I have been working." What a powerful truth. Could it be that Jesus saw visions of the Father performing miracles, then copied His example and saw the miracles taking place?

Invading the earth with the Kingdom of God will and can only come about if we position ourselves in such a way that we can fill it with what we see and know. God has given us the blueprints and strategy—we need to do the stuff, and to get out there with the Gospel of power.

We are in the season of the at-hand Kingdom of God. It's up to you to reach out and receive it in hand. When you possess the Kingdom, the King possesses you. Change is coming—it's a forceful change, and it comes from Heaven at hand. This change is like a mighty and powerful wind in strength and might, and it will sweep, invade, and fill the land with the Gospel of the Kingdom. The King *is* indeed coming, but with our supernatural power and strength, with our heart and our spirit, we can truly cry out, "The King is here

…He's here…He lives…He's in me and I'm in Him, and together we shall invade the earth with His glory."

Embark on a mission to manifest the Kingdom of God in your corner of the earth. Don't be content with the old patterns but press in for the new. Gather with like-minded believers who desire to shake the mountains and transform the world with the supernatural power of the Kingdom to heal and restore it.

It's an adventure, most assuredly, but it's a lot more exciting than anything in the natural realm because there are no limitations in the spiritual realm. Because you live and have your being in Him, and because He lives in you, every square inch of the world that you tread can be filled and overtaken with His glory.

KINGDOM STRATEGY

- Birth the harvest—pray in the Spirit in the midnight hours.

- When you receive a prophetic word, become a sign of the prophetic word you've received. Hear it, speak it, live it.

- It's not prideful to ask God for big things. Think big, dream big! First and always, though, seek to grow in favor with Him through the relentless pursuit of Him.

- Consider Kingdom hindrances, such as disobedience. Prayerfully ask the Holy Spirit to reveal anything in your life that hinders you from increasing and filling your radius or sphere of influence with the glory of the Lord.

- Take care of the poor, the needy, and the afflicted. Proclaim liberty to captives and recovery of sight to the blind. Pray and speak the Word.

- Pray and ask God for the masses and multitudes!

PERSONAL PRAYER

Father, I thank You for the Holy Spirit, for the authority that is Your Word. Lord, I'm dreaming big—I want to be a laborer; I want to see men, women, young people, and children reached with the Gospel of Jesus Christ. I want to see the invasion of the Kingdom of God in the earth, to see it increase and manifest for Your glory and end-time purposes. Oh, Lord of the harvest, anoint me to proclaim Your Gospel in towns, cities, and nations. I want revival not only in my life and heart, but in my family, in my neighborhood. In the past, I've waited with expectation for the Kingdom, but I want the Kingdom now. I waited in expectation of harvest, but I want it now. Forgive me for being of the future mindset and blind to what's happening now. Thank You for Your increase of grace and favor over my life. Help me to rend the heavens, to create atmospheres and new places, Lord, where those who tread after I've been there will experience open heavens. This city, my family, our nation, Father, all belong to You! The earth is Yours and the fullness thereof and all who dwell in it. Give me the harvest fire Lord—Kingdom fire—the desire to build, to fill, to demonstrate, to preach, to teach, to advance the truth of Your Word in power. Give me a vision and release Your fire. Burden my heart for the lost, the captive, the oppressed. Here I am, Lord. Send me. Release Your Kingdom into our midst—let it come. Anoint me to preach the good news. Give me Your keys and strategies to win nations. Make me a walking flame of passion for the lost. Thank You Father! In Jesus' precious name, amen.

Endnotes

1. Trent C. Butler ed., *Holman Bible Dictionary* (1991), s.v. "Bethel," http://www.studylight.org/dic/hbd/view.cgi?number=T892 (accessed 25 June 2008).

2. Matthew Henry, *Matthew Henry Commentary on the Whole Bible* (Peabody, MA: Hendrickson Publishers, 1991), 1706, http://www.studylight.org/com/mhc-com/view.cgi?book=jer&chapter=001 (accessed 25 June 2008).

3. Ibid.

CHAPTER 5

SIGNS OF THE KINGDOM IN YOUR MIDST

This chapter serves as a quick reinforcement helper to what you've learned about the Kingdom thus far. It's a handy reference for you, a great tool to look back on when the Kingdom seems invisible to you in the spirit. The Kingdom is never far away—it's in you, it's in me, it's Jesus. Jesus is enthroned in your heart; the King of kings and Lord of lords is reigning and ruling there.

THE KINGDOM OF GOD IS JESUS CHRIST

Most of the Pharisees never realized that the Kingdom of God was in their midst, embodied as Jesus Christ of Nazareth. He invaded their world and they didn't even know it. Ignorantly they asked Jesus when the Kingdom of God was coming. He didn't ridicule them with His answer but rather said, "The Kingdom of God does not come with observation; nor will they say, 'See here!' or 'See there!' For indeed, the Kingdom of God is within you" (Luke 17:20b-21).

He was telling them that the Kingdom of God wasn't something to gawk at or point at, but it was among them.

The Spirit of God anointed Jesus before He accomplished the works that the Father gave Him to do. Hundreds of years before the birth of Jesus, the prophet Isaiah prophesied concerning the Lord Jesus being anointed by the Spirit of the Lord. Eventually, at the appointed time, Jesus read this prophecy from Isaiah 61:1-2 to His Jewish brethren in the synagogue. Can you visualize the scene? Jesus steps up, takes the scroll, and reads the portion that identifies Him as more than just the son of Joseph and Mary. He is saying that He is the Anointed One! The following account was recorded by the apostle Luke:

> *So He came to Nazareth, where He had been brought up. And as His custom was, He went into the synagogue on the Sabbath day, and stood up to read. And He was handed the book of the prophet Isaiah. And when He had opened the book, He found the place where it was written: "The Spirit of the Lord is upon Me, because He has anointed Me to preach the Gospel to the poor; He has sent Me to heal the brokenhearted, to proclaim liberty to the captives and recovery of sight to the blind, to set at liberty those who are oppressed; to proclaim the acceptable year of the Lord" (Luke 4:16-19).*

There are many kinds of anointing referred to in this passage, but before we examine them, I want to point out two of them that are essential and foundational for the growth of any anointing. "God anointed Jesus of Nazareth with the Holy Spirit and with power, who went about doing good and healing all who were oppressed by the devil, for God was with Him" (Acts 10:38). Here we see Jesus with the anointing of the Holy Spirit and the anointing of power. Clearly there is a distinction because the power of God is not the Holy Spirit. The power of God is what the Holy Spirit brings.

Some positions and areas of responsibility that must flow out of the anointing of the Holy Spirit and the anointing of power I list below with supporting Scriptures:

- Pastor anointing (see Eph. 4:11-16)

- Teacher anointing (see Eph. 4:11-16)

- Worship and song anointing (see 1 Chron. 15:16; 25:1-7)

- Intercession anointing (see Prov. 31:9; Gen. 18:23-33)

- Apostolic anointing (see Titus 1:1)

- Prophetic anointing (see Rom. 12:6)

- Apostolic business anointing (see Gen. 41:37-41)

- Anointing for administration (see 1 Kings 3:10-14)

- Giving anointing (see Prov. 11:25; Mark 12:42-44)

- Craftsmanship skills anointing (see Exod. 36:1,2; Zech. 1:20)

The anointing of the Holy Spirit and the anointing of power come upon our lives when we fulfill three conditions:

1. When we are walking in holiness

2. When we are walking in an attitude of repentance and cleansing

3. When we are planted in the house of God

Before the power of God comes, we must apply the Blood of Jesus first for protection over our lives and over our households. When the Blood is applied, God will bring His power. When we're anointing with the presence of God, He will anoint us with the power.

THE KINGDOM OF GOD DEMONSTRATES HIS POWER

I have covered most of this in Chapter 3, "Demonstration of the Kingdom," and will emphasize it throughout the book; however, I want to include it again here because I can't illuminate this enough. So many churches, particularly in the Western world, end services without a demonstration of the power of God, especially as it relates to healing and deliverance. It's too bad. Preaching is good, but rarely do we see the demonstration following the preaching of the Gospel. The apostle Paul said that this speech and preaching "were not with persuasive words of human wisdom, but in demonstration of the Spirit and of power, that your faith should not be in the wisdom of men but in the power of God" (1 Cor. 2:4-5).

Often preachers teach the Kingdom, and they bring people to a place where they have faith to receive, but the preachers don't go on to demonstrate the power of God. Instead they say things like, "Let's wait until the evangelist gets here. Todd Bentley has the gift of healing, so let's have him pray for the sick. I'm just a pastor (or a teacher, or a prophet). I don't do signs and wonders."

They don't do signs and wonders, and yet they preach and teach? Does that emulate what Christ did? He was a teacher and a healer. He taught and He healed—the two went hand-in-hand. God's Word and power were partners. The Gospel is preaching, teaching, and healing. Jesus never presented the Gospel without signs and wonders. Every person who preaches or teaches or witnesses should venture into the demonstration of the Word and heal every sickness and every disease just as Jesus did. Jesus said that whoever believes in Him would not only do the same works that He did, but they would do even greater works than He accomplished (see John 14:12).

THE KINGDOM OF GOD CASTS OUT DEMONS

We know the Kingdom of God is in our midst when we're casting out devils. Jesus told the Pharisees that if He cast out demons with the finger of God then surely the Kingdom of God has come upon us (see Luke 11:20).

In Africa, we found that a supernatural encounter in the realm of good and evil spirits is a very common phenomenon. African people believe in the invisible world and are quite sensitive to spirits, both good and evil. We often see men and women bound by demons because of personal or generational involvement with witchcraft and sorcery. On one particular crusade evening in Ethiopia, the ushers brought a young woman of about 20 years of age to the stage along with her mother. This woman had been unable to walk normally for over 15 years because her feet were bound with shackles.

Like the demoniac in the Bible, left unbound she turned into a raving maniac, beating people up and sometimes attempting suicide. To prevent her from killing others or herself, family members had no choice but to bind her feet with chains.

I was prompted by the Holy Spirit and exhorted all of the Fresh Fire team and local pastors to corporately declare repeatedly, "Holy is the Lord! Holy is the Lord!" Within moments, the spiritual atmosphere changed, charged with the presence of God, and so I told the young woman that she needed to receive Jesus Christ into her heart and to acknowledge Him as her Lord, and she did. The FFM team and I broke the power of generational witchcraft over her and her family tree and then cast out devils with the Word of God. We asked the young woman's mother for the key to unlock the chains and set her free. Reluctantly, because of her own fear, she handed over the keys, hoping not to see a violent outbreak. When the lock was undone, the young woman praised the Lord and lifted her hands in jubilation. Her mother fell to her knees and wept, unable to contain her joy.

This daughter, bound with chains and tormented by demons for

15 years, was set free by the power of Jesus Christ. He is the same yesterday, today, and forever (see Heb. 13:8). Yes, greater is Jesus in us than he that is in the world (see 1 John 4:4)! Jesus has come to set the captives free. This is a true sign of the Kingdom in our midst!

THE KINGDOM OF GOD IS MARKED BY MIRACLES

The Kingdom of God demonstrates healing the sick and setting the captives free. When the Kingdom of God breaks in, poverty turns into prosperity and sickness turns into health. Redemption happens, sinful areas in our lives are cleansed, and we begin to walk in holiness. When the Kingdom of God invades our world, it becomes as it is in Heaven here on earth. Miracles happen.

Visible miracles are evidence of the Kingdom of God at work. When John the Baptist was in prison, he sent his disciples to ask Jesus if He was the Coming One or if there was someone else coming (see Matt. 11:3). Jesus answered John's disciples and said, "Go and tell John the things which you hear and see: The blind see and the lame walk; the lepers are cleansed and the deaf hear; the dead are raised up and the poor have the gospel preached to them" (Matt. 11:4-5).

Jesus was saying that the Kingdom of God is at hand and in our midst when we see the evidence. The signs and wonders of the manifestation of the Kingdom of God are that the lame walk, the blind see, the dead are raised, the poor have the Gospel preached to them, and the deaf hear. How much more proof of the Kingdom do we need?

THE KINGDOM OF GOD IS "CHRIST IN YOU, THE HOPE OF GLORY"

We know the Kingdom of God is in our midst when people hear the message of the Gospel and they experience the new birth—they are born again. Jesus said "Unless one is born again, he cannot see the Kingdom of God" (John 3:3). He also said, "Unless one is born of water and the Spirit, he cannot enter the Kingdom of God" (John 3:5).

The Kingdom of God is in our midst when the harvest is reaped because we get filled up with the passion of Jesus Christ and then we go into the world to preach the Gospel. "Christ in you, the hope of glory" (Col. 1:27b). We want to be radical believers who reflect Jesus in our good characters as we release the power of God in the world. We know that Jesus wasn't subject to the laws of science or medicine, fabricated laws and orders, poverty and the restrictions or limitations of the world system. Though He lived on the earth, His Kingdom was not of the earth's realm (see John 18:36). Likewise, we who are born again of the Spirit of the living God and who have Jesus Christ in us also live in a higher realm (see John 3:6).

Like Jesus, we realize that our Kingdom is not of this world and that our "citizenship is in Heaven" (Philippians 3:20). But while we're here on earth, God wants us, the Body of Christ, to demonstrate His power to the lost so that they will be saved. The Kingdom of God advances in the earth when we live with the awareness that we are the expression of Jesus Christ to lost humanity. His hands are our hands, His message is our message, and His burning love for the unsaved becomes our passion. His Kingdom invades our world because He is the master strategist. It's all because of Jesus Christ, and He is in us.

Part II

KINGSHIP

CHAPTER 6

KINGDOM DOMINION

God has entrusted to us the ministry of the Kingdom. That is, the advancing of the Kingdom by exercising our authority in Christ Jesus as stewards of everything that goes on in this realm called earth. Everything that exists is from God, and we administrate it from His hand. David enumerated God's preeminence, His regency, and His authority to rule in his beautiful thanksgiving tribute to God in First Chronicles, as the people brought offerings to God to the temple, because God is He who created the heavens and the earth, the One who is before all things.

> *But who am I, and who are my people, that we should be able to offer so willingly as this? For all things come from You, and of Your own we have given You* (1 Chronicles 29:14).

DELEGATED STEWARDSHIP

God's authority to rule is His pre-existence and His holiness. He was before creation. "The heaven, even the heavens are the Lord's;

but the earth He has given to the children of men" (Ps. 115:16). God's will decides and designs. God's Word creates, and His works are a demonstration of the Holy Spirit's power. The Holy Spirit, our partner, displays God's will, but we administrate it. Our authority to rule is in God's authority. He has delegated to us and has invited us to partner in administrating everything that He has in His hand. He has crowned us with glory and honor and has made us to have dominion over the works of His hands, placing all things under our feet. The duties are ours and the results are God's. Do you understand your Kingdom duties? Do you understand your responsibilities and the consequences of them? Do you understand who you are, what you have, and the significance of all of this? It's so much to absorb, and even King David wondered in amazement:

> *When I consider Your heavens, the work of Your fingers, the moon and the stars, which You have ordained, what is man that You are mindful of him, and the son of man that You visit him? For You have made him a little lower than the angels, and You have crowned him with glory and honor. You have made him to have dominion over the works of Your hands; You have put all things under his feet, all sheep and oxen—even the beasts of the field, the birds of the air, and the fish of the sea that pass through the paths of the seas. O Lord, our Lord, how excellent is Your name in all the earth* (Psalm 8:3-9).

God has delegated the stewardship of the Earth to us. The heavens, even the heavens of Heaven are the Lord's, but He has given the Earth to the children of men. We're responsible for everything—including sin and thus sickness, disease, poverty, and death. We cry out to God for help, and He responds as He did for Moses whenever Moses cried out for help. Essentially His response always was: "Why do you cry to Me? Stretch forth your rod. The authority, Moses, is in your hand. I have made you a steward to have dominion over all the works of My hands. You and every person are responsible for the mess in the world, and you're accountable now for filling the earth with the knowledge of the glory of the Lord, taking dominion over sin, sickness, disease, poverty, and death. I have entrusted the earth to you; I give you the duties, and I give you the power. We are partners. The duties are yours, and the results are Mine."

This is your earth. This is our earth. We are responsible for the spiritual climate and atmosphere wherever we live, wherever we travel, wherever we go. The kingdoms of the world belong to the Kingdom of our Lord and Christ—they just don't know it yet, that's why God is sending you into the far reaches of the earth to proclaim the Gospel of the Kingdom of God that is invincible and the only true Kingdom.

It's a hefty responsibility, isn't it? Yet many believers don't take it seriously. We simply have to take ownership of who we are as sons and daughters of God and embrace the revelation of the authority and the dominion of the Kingdom to advance and war against sickness, disease, poverty, and death.

In the beginning, we had dominion—a natural dominion over fish, birds, and every beast and creeping thing—but it wasn't a spiritual dominion. God gave us a boundary and a limit to our dominion, which was the Garden. Sin destroyed the partnership that we had with God in His creation, but now, in redemption, we partner with God's wisdom, power, and Kingdom in the re-establishment of God's rule over all of our circumstances and situations. Think of His wisdom, His power, His Word! We get to partner with God now in the re-establishment of His Kingdom concerning *every* circumstance and *every* situation. He has given the earth to you and to me. He wants us to take our place and to understand that we have duties and that God does the results.

Yes, we gave up our dominion one time in the Garden, but God restored it to us right after the Flood (see Gen. 9). Our spiritual dominion came in Christ, and now we have dominion over demonic powers and principalities, spiritual hosts of wickedness, sin, disease, death, and poverty.

HERE AM I, SEND ME!

Do you know who you are and what you have? You can't exercise authority and dominion to advance the Kingdom of God unless you do. "For the earnest expectation of the creation eagerly waits for the revealing of the *sons of God*. For the creation was subjected to futility" (Rom. 8:19-20a). Death, decay, and corruption came to the earth because the sons of God sinned. Even creation is under the curse. Not only is man under the curse, but the earth is too because of our sin. We must take responsibility. How do we do that? As we live in the glorious liberty of God's Spirit, which is the glory of God, the more and more creation becomes free from its own death, corruption, and decay: "…because the creation itself also will be delivered from the bondage of corruption into the glorious liberty of the children of God" (Rom. 8:21). Freedom won't ultimately be fulfilled until we are redeemed in body, at the Second Coming of Jesus. The more we arise and shine, "for your light has come," and as we experience the liberty of God's Spirit, we actually remove the curse of death, decay, and corruption.

Not only the Church, but also even the Earth itself waits for the day in which the sons of God will take their place and dominion and remove the curse. We look to God when we see a spiritual captive in bondage, or a nation in darkness, but do you know that God looks to us and says, "Arise, shine; for your light has come! And the glory of the Lord is risen upon you" (Isa. 60:1-3)?

The Bible promises a day in which the knowledge of the glory of the Lord shall cover the earth as the waters cover the sea (see Hab. 2:14). Is God going to do that in His sovereignty, or do we have partnership in bringing about the knowledge of the glory of the Lord? How is that glory going to come?

We have this glory as treasures in earthen vessels (see 2 Cor. 3:7). We fill the earth with the knowledge of the glory of the Lord as we take ground for Christ. As we take ground, we advance the Kingdom and take territory with the Gospel. Once the Gospel reaches all of the nations of the earth, the end will come.

Take Your Place

So back to that question: will God sovereignly cover the earth with His glory or is He waiting for us to say, "Here I am Lord, send me!" Is He also waiting for us to say, "Send me, I'm *going*?" Many of us wait for sovereign God to do it all on a sovereign day and time. We rely on Him to save the day, and we wait for that day and the Rapture. However, God is waiting for us to take our place by knowing who we are and knowing what we have, in order to advance for Him, because He has entrusted us as stewards concerning the earth where we have dominion. Our attitude should be: "The earth is ours, let's clean up the mess!"

That's my attitude in ministry. Real power, signs, wonders, and miracles started to work, flow, and function in my ministry when I stopped asking God what He was going to do about things and set out to ask Him what *I* could do about things with the authority He'd given me. I'd travel to Africa and encounter oppression by witch doctors and principalities of witchcraft and I'd ask, "Oh God, what are You going to do?" He'd say, "Todd, what are *you* going to do about all this?"

Do you remember when the disciples were in the boat and tossed by the storm (see Mark 4:35-41)? The winds and the waves beat against the boat and the disciples feared for their lives, but I believe Jesus waited because He wanted to see what they would do—if they would take authority over the storm, which *He* finally did.

Do you remember reading about that man, crippled from birth, in Acts 3? Peter and John encountered him while heading toward the temple at the hour of prayer, the ninth hour. Peter told the man, "Look at us," and the man did, giving them his attention, expecting to receive something from *them*. Peter said, "Silver and gold I do not have, but what I do have I give you: in the name of Jesus Christ of Nazareth, rise up and walk" (Acts 3:6).

Who was responsible for the miracle? Was it God or Peter taking dominion? Don't be too quick to answer. Yes, God ultimately was responsible, but Peter exercised the authority given to him in the absence of Jesus. Peter was saying, "Silver and gold have I none, but I can tell you that I know what I have, and what I do have I am responsible for, because it has been given to me because He is gone."

It is to our advantage that He goes so that the Holy Spirit can come. Christ says, "He who believes in Me, the works that I do he will do also…" (John 14:12). The model of ministry today is the model of the relationship that Jesus and the Father had, except that now it's you and the Father doing the works that Christ did.

If Jesus saw a man with no arm, what would He do or say? Would He say, "Help, God, I ask for a new arm for this man" or would He say, "Stretch forth your arm and be healed"? His pattern was the latter, and so it should be for us. God has given us the power, the authority, and the duty.

It's Our Responsibility

Is it possible that you or I can release the healing anointing? Can we just go into a city, have a healing service, and expect healings, or do we have to wait, pray, and fast about it for a week first? Understand this truth. Jesus gave the disciples power and authority and said, "As you go, preach saying the kingdom of heaven is at hand. Heal the sick, cleanse the leper, raise the dead, cast out devils" (Matt. 10:7). You don't have to ask God, "Is it Your will to heal the sick? Is it Your will to use me in healing? Do You want miracles in this place? Do You want miracles, Lord, in the nation?"

God gave them the power and the authority once, and then He said "Go ye" (see Mark 16:15 KJV). Those words meant, "Act like you really know who you are. Believe that you are who I said you are and that you can really do what I said you could do. Whatever city or town you enter, heal the sick there. I've made it your responsibility now."

The healing ministry is our responsibility now. If you went and prayed for the sick this moment, people would be healed because silver and gold you do not have, but what you do have... (see Acts 3:6). Do you know what you do have? Do you know who you are so that you can use what you have? Peter did. "What I do have I give you: in the name of Jesus Christ of Nazareth, rise up and walk" (Acts 3:6b).

Do you know that people are blessed when you are in their midst? You are a son or daughter of God—one of the sons or daughters of God. Laban said, "I am blessed because Jacob is here" (see Gen. 30:27). Laban knew who Jacob was and what he had. Pharaoh was blessed because Joseph was there. Africa was blessed because I was there. This isn't arrogance or pride; this is just knowing who you are. Your church is blessed because you are there. How can anything be the same if you or I or any other son or daughter of God is there? How can your work be the same? How can your government be the same? We carry the glory; the glory transforms.

Wherever you go, you go as an ambassador of the Kingdom of God—as an ambassador for Christ. Things will change, not only because God will do them sovereignly, but because you take your place with what God has already given you.

When we enter into a foreign country and see people in darkness, we have to realize that we (humankind) are responsible for the sin in that country, even though it's not our own country. The wars, the deaths, and the famines aren't God's fault; they're ours because of the sin in the Garden. God has given us dominion, though, to do something about the mess. We carry the power and the authority, the very presence of God into those dark areas. We have to believe that we've received and then act appropriately. Yes, you can heal the sick in the darkest country. Jesus told us that whatever city or town we were to enter, we should heal the sick there (see Matt. 10:7-8). So that gives us a choice—to either do it, or not to do it. However, God has entrusted us to do it as our part in our partnership. If you want a healing service, have one. There's no need to ask God if He's going to show up with miracles. There's no need to ask God if He can heal through you. Lay hands on the sick, and they will recover. Jesus said that all power and authority was given to Him in Heaven and on earth and to "go therefore…" (see Matt. 28:18-19). So go therefore!

WHAT ARE YOU GOING TO DO?

Let's go back to that windy boat scene from Matthew 8:23-27. Jesus gave the disciples sailing orders to depart to the other side of the sea of Tiberias into the country of Gadara, which lay east of Jordan. The winds blew, the disciples thought they would surely die, and they couldn't believe that Jesus could sleep through it. "Help us!" they cried, "Master, Teacher, don't You care that we're perishing?" Isn't that just like us? If we don't get an immediate response from God, we assume the worst—that He doesn't care about us, or perhaps that we've sinned or that God's mad at us. It's easy to interpret things this way when our lives get tough. Jesus awoke and rebuked the winds saying, "Peace, be still," and immediately the waters calmed. Then, Jesus rebuked their unbelief. What Jesus was saying was, "It's not that it's not My will that you have breakthrough in your storms…what I really wanted was for you to have revelation of who I am and who you are in Me, and I hoped you'd do something about the storm yourself. But you didn't. I had to do it."

Jesus could sleep through it all because of His security and understanding of His authority; He knew who He was. He had hoped the disciples would have an understanding of it all, but they didn't. When they said, "Help…don't You care," it was like admitting that they didn't know who they were and who was in the boat. I know people who have been Christians for 25 years and yet still don't understand those things. God has been faithful, has healed them, has blessed them, and yet they still cry out asking God what He's going to do. How many rescues does it take before we genuinely realize who we are and the authority we have to rebuke the wind ourselves? Do you have a storm in your life right now, a difficult situation that's making you think the worst (that perhaps God doesn't love you) or that's causing you to search for answers as to why He hasn't yet delivered you of it? Could it be He wants you to have revelation of who you are and to do something about your storm? God is waiting for you to take dominion. He'll deliver you from your storms, but there's a time or a storm coming where He is going to say, "What are *you* going to do?"

TAKING DOMINION IN AFRICA

I was in Africa, about to preach in my first crusade in Uganda. I wanted it to be successful, but a particular witchdoctor in the crowd did everything he could to close us down. He called in big, dark, angry clouds and rain with his witchcraft and incantations, and everyone wondered what to do about the downpour as everything turned to mud and muck around our makeshift outdoors setup. However, something in my spirit told me to take authority over the storm and the witchdoctor rather than to cry out to God for help. Oh, believe me, I wanted to cry out to God and ask Him why He'd allow such a thing to happen at such a time and so on and so on, but I didn't! I knew in my heart that, at that point, if I didn't beat the storm, the devil would lick me every time I had a crusade in Africa.

I challenged the fellow publicly and said, "You will not operate in your witchcraft!" He said something back in a weird demonic-like tongue. Then I bound and rebuked that witch-doctor, the rain, and the clouds. "I said, 'Rain I bind you. Clouds I rebuke you. Sky I command you: clear in the mighty name of Jesus!'" The clouds parted, the rains stopped, the sky turned blue, and 10,000 people returned to hear the Gospel. Oh, and one more thing—the witchdoctor gave his heart to the Lord. Had I not taken dominion and used my authority in Christ Jesus this break-through may not have happened.

The next time I went to Uganda, the devil really wanted to challenge my authority, and he gathered his minions. The first night of this crusade was the worst ever—it rained and stormed even heavier this time, and there wasn't one but 1,800 witchdoctors in this one meeting. Although it had been perfectly sunny all day, a dark angry cloud rolled in over the crusade just before we were to start. I knew something was up because for several mornings the sound of a witchdoctor chanting and casting curses upon our team could be heard coming from across the other side of the river near our hotel.

Things were getting rougher and more threatening by the moment, and some of my team asked me when I was going to do something about it, as I'd done at that previous crusade. "Are you just going to let this go on, Todd? Are you just going to let the devil wash out the crusade?" But the Lord said, "Not yet—wait." That night we saw only 76 saved. It may seem like a lot, but we're used to 5,000 souls in one night!

The following day I prayed all day long and cried out to God for help. Only now can I imagine Him rolling His eyes and asking back, "Why do you cry out to Me? You know what to do"—but I hadn't thought of that yet. That evening another dark, angry cloud rolled in at precisely the same time, 4:45 P.M. That night we saw a hundred out of 12,000 people saved. By now though, we should have seen thousands of souls saved at the very least. My target was 70,000 for the whole span of the crusade; however, we had a long way to go at only 176 salvations.

Day three arrived, and after again praying all day, the Lord instructed me to fast. "Today," He said, "I will give you the spirit of Elijah." So I fasted, and guess what? I arrived at the crusade at 4:30 and no sign of the dark cloud. I'm thinking, *Hallelujah! I got breakthrough!* With God as my witness, at 4:45 P.M., I stepped out onto the platform, and the moment I grabbed the mike, a dark, angry cloud blew in and poured buckets of rain on us. The crowd scattered, and I got an electrical shock from the microphone. I thought about all the witchdoctors out there probably laughing. Can you imagine, three days of the devil driving everything away?

Finally, God said, "How much longer are you going to take this?" With determined resolve, I answered, "I'm done. I'm exercising authority!"

I got down to business: "In the name of Jesus, I take authority over the powers of witchcraft...If you are under the power of witchcraft, if you are a witchdoctor, if you are sorcerer, get down here now!" We counted 1,800 people who ran to the altar. The moment I broke the power of witchcraft off them, down they went, manifesting demons like snakes in a giant snake pit. At that precise time, the skies cleared and a double rainbow appeared. Over the next three days, 34,000 got saved. Wow. From 176 souls to 34,000 because I took dominion.

The devil knows he's not going to get me with a storm in Africa again because I passed the test, and he knows that I know who I am and what I can do with what I have because of who I know.

MIRACLES AND RESPONSIBILITY

One time I prayed for the deaf and I said, "Oh God. The deaf. Oh, help me." I prayed and they heard. The next time I went to pray for a group of deaf people and called out to God for help, He said, "That's enough! I did something about it the last time. Now I'm holding you responsible with what you've seen to do it this time."

Miracles carry responsibility. Every time you see one, God expects more of you the next time. Do you pass the first test? I did, and hundreds of deaf ears have opened. The more that God is faithful to perform His miracles before you, the more He holds you responsible to take dominion the next time yourself.

If you're going through a storm right now, perhaps God is waiting for you because of how much you have seen Him deliver you of already. Take dominion over your own storm. Don't give your authority over to the devil, and don't let him orchestrate your life. If you take authority but nothing happens, perhaps something in your life is hindering things.

HINDRANCES TO AUTHORITY

Here are six hindrances to watch for.

#1 *Lack of Intimacy with God*

How well do you know the Father? How much time do you spend in His presence, in that quiet place of His presence, seeking to know Him and to know His ways? How much time do you spend in the Word? There is no way you can have the assurance of who you are in Him and of who He is in you if you don't know Him. If you don't know Him, you can't hear Him, and you won't know what to do. How can you see what the Father is doing, as Jesus did, if you don't spend time with Him in a quiet place? Jesus often withdrew to quiet places to be alone with the Father preceding great miracles. Why was that? When you spend time with Him, you'll learn how to recognize His voice, which is vital for Kingdom dominion.

#2 *Disobedience: Not Doing the Will of God*

"Your kingdom come. Your will be done on earth as it is in heaven" (Matt. 6:10). In other words, let the Kingdom of God and the reign of God come as His will done on earth. True Kingdom authority comes out of doing the will of God. God will entrust to us the Kingdom and the manifestation of it to the extent that we are obedient and faithful to His law and Word. The key to the will of God is "I only do those things that I see the Father doing" (see John 5:19). If we are willing and obedient, we will eat the good of the land. God will entrust the Kingdom of God and the manifestation of the Kingdom to your life to the extent that you are faithful to God's Word.

"Your will be done…" is surrender. To do the will of God means that you need to see and hear what the Father is doing and saying. We give the devil authority by being disobedient to what we see and hear. We're not only disobedient to the *rhema* word, or spoken word, but to His written Word—perhaps even more so—and yet we expect authority and victory.

You have to believe the Word of God and act on it. The Kingdom of God showed up in my ministry in power when I believed in His Word and stopped praying for God to do what He already told me He'd do. That's when I believed who God said He was and who He said I was, and I acted as one who knew without a doubt that it was so, and then I took my rightful place.

#3 *Unforgiveness*

"And forgive us our debts, as we forgive our debtors" (Matt. 6:12). Right in the context of inviting the Kingdom, God talks about the importance of forgiving and receiving forgiveness. Offense and unforgiveness hinders the manifestation of Kingdom power. There's no unforgiveness in Heaven. Can you forgive yourself? Have you forgiven others? Is there someone you're still resentful of? If you cannot forgive, you may lose that dominion and authority and wonder why things aren't happening the way they should.

#4 Giving Place to the Devil

Have you given place to the devil? Are there any open doors, inroads, avenues, or opportunities? Paul says, "nor give place to the devil" (Eph. 4:27). Is there any hidden sin, unconfessed sin? Any little sin that you think you're getting away with? Does the devil have anything on you? "Stand fast therefore in the liberty by which Christ has made us free, and do not be entangled again with a yoke of bondage" (Gal. 5:1).

#5 Lack of Meekness/Surrender

What or who rules your life or heart? Your work? The computer? The world? Or does Jesus rule and reign in it? If you're not submitting everything to Him, to the Kingship of Jesus, you can't expect a great manifestation of the Kingdom in your kingdom radius or sphere. True surrender is saying, "Your will be done. I give it all to You, Jesus—I lay it all at the Cross, no matter the cost, because I'm confident that you will make things right."

#6 A Kingdom Divided Against Itself

This could tie in somewhat with #4, but pride too gets in the mix here to cause disunity, division, disloyalty, disinterest, and a gamut of other manifestations. Jesus tells us that a kingdom divided against itself is brought to desolation and that every city or house divided against itself will not stand (see Matt. 12:25). Jesus removes any illusions about any neutrality with regard to His ministry—if we aren't for Him, we are against Him, as He says: "He who is not with Me is against Me, and he who does not gather with Me scatters abroad" (Matt. 12:30).

We can't serve God and something else—like, say, money. We can't walk in the spirit and walk in the flesh. Do you know what happened when satan fell—what got him kicked out of the Kingdom? Pride—a Kingdom divided against itself. Check your pride—does it divide you? Check your heart too, because anything that's in it that is contrary to the Word and the Spirit of God actually divides the Kingdom and causes its fall within you. What does your heart say; what does your life show? How many "I love God, buts" are there? You love God, but you love money. You love God, but you love the flesh. You love God, but you have unforgiveness. You love God, but you have envy. You love God, but you love gossip. These are signs of a divided heart, and they destroy your own authority. Your heart in one way is loyal and submitted to the Lordship of Jesus, but in another way, you're doing your own thing. A Kingdom divided against itself can not stand. You have to have a loyal heart, and I challenge you to ask, "What's going on in the rooms and chambers of my heart?"

Do you know what satan came to offer to Jesus? The kingdoms of the world! Why did the devil do that? Because he could. They belonged to him. Hear this though; God has given the earth to you. If you're going for one of satan's kingdoms, your life, as Jesus said, will be one of ultimate unhappiness.

Listen, these are all things that are vital if we're to exercise dominion in the world. Pray and ask the Holy Spirit to reveal to you those things that are hindering the manifestation of the Kingdom around you, because this list is by no means exhaustive. Jesus did every miracle as an anointed Man and not as God, and He had to overcome the world, just as you and I have to. We do it first by spending time with God, and His glory alone will illuminate the darkness in our lives.

Jesus had the Spirit without measure as a man, and every miracle He performed as a man, as the Son of God. The same temptations cross our paths, yet Christ remained without sin. The Bible says that He *became* obedient. Christ had to work at it, just as we do. How does the Spirit without measure come to us? Jesus modeled to us the unlimited anointing that came about by obedience. Obedience to the Father's will is the key to the unlimited anointing. What is God telling you to do, what is He saying, where is He directing you? Do it. The advancement of the Kingdom depends on it, as does inheriting the riches of the Kingdom.

INHERITING VS. ENTERING THE KINGDOM

The meek shall inherit the earth. The Bible says this in both the Old and New Testaments (see Ps. 37:11). The one we're most familiar with is in the Beatitudes, given as the Sermon on the Mount (see Matt. 5:5). This passage says, "Blessed *are* the meek, for they *shall* inherit the earth." In the Greek, "meek" translates as showing a willingness to submit and work under proper authority and showing a willingness to disregard one's own "rights" and privileges.[1] The meek person in the Old Testament translation was not one to be pushed around. It referred to a person with strength *under control*, as a strong stallion trained to do the job instead of running wild.[2]

Believers must be willing to first submit and work under God's authority with a devout willingness to give up their own rights or privileges in pursuit of doing God's will. We are able to do this because of our confidence in God to protect our interests and causes. God promises to the meek that He will not allow us to be short-changed; far from it, in fact, because He says the meek shall *inherit* the earth. That's a great reward, don't you think?

It's one thing to *enter* into the Kingdom, but it's another thing to *inherit* it now. Yes, we get to enter into the Kingdom and live there because we have said "Yes" to Christ and we are born of the Spirit and we will go to Heaven, but what will your inheritance be in the Kingdom today? If you're not willing to submit, how much of the Kingdom can God entrust you with?

Paul says:

> *Do you not know that the saints will judge the world? And if the world will be judged by you, are you unworthy to judge the smallest matters? Do you not know that we shall judge angels? How much more, things that pertain to this life?* (1 Corinthians 6:2-3).

And when Peter asks Jesus what he and the disciples will get for giving up everything to follow Him, Jesus replies:

> *Assuredly I say to you, that in the regeneration, when the Son of Man sits on the throne of His glory, you who have followed Me will also sit on twelve thrones, judging the twelve tribes of Israel. And everyone who has left*

houses or brothers or sisters or father or mother or wife or children or lands, for My name's sake, shall receive a hundredfold, and inherit eternal life. But many who are first will be last, and the last first (Matthew 19:28-30).

We will judge the world, and will judge angels, and there will be honor for those who sacrifice for Jesus' sake. Whatever you've given up for Him will be returned to you a hundred times over, *in addition to inheriting eternal life.*

Now the works of the flesh are evident, which are: adultery, fornication, uncleanness, lewdness, idolatry, sorcery, hatred, contentions, jealousies, outbursts of wrath, selfish ambitions, dissensions, heresies, envy, murders, drunkenness, revelries, and the like; of which I tell you beforehand, just as I also told you in time past, that those who practice such things will not inherit the kingdom of God (Galatians 5:19-21).

There's inference, therefore, when we string these passages together, that there are those who will enter in and see the Kingdom, but not necessarily inherit things—not judge, not rule and reign. God desires us to partner with Him in the administration of the Kingdom, whether it's here on earth, in the millennium, or in the Kingdom of God forever. There will be ones who will be a part of God's divine heavenly court system: those who will not only see and enter, but also inherit the Kingdom.

Some believers will enter the Kingdom, but not inherit it

because of carnality. They will make it to Heaven, yes, but never up close to the throne with Him because they've lived too much by the works of the flesh, thereby not storing up treasures in Heaven. I believe there are regions in Heaven where those people whose lives have reflected the glory of God on earth will reside closer to the glory of God nearer to the throne, but that's fodder for another book.

As believers, we get to see the Kingdom of Heaven now on the earth in measure and to enter in as our final destination, but do you know what else I want? I want to inherit it! I want to participate with Christ in ruling and reigning in the Kingdom. He has invited you and me to that place of authority here and now as we see the Kingdom. Why settle for so much less when God has so much more? Why stand on the sidelines as you watch others receive breakthrough? I challenge you to be a breaker. Get your own breakthrough! Stop partaking of the blessings of the breakthroughs of others and taste of the blessings firsthand. Someone else's leftovers aren't nearly as good as reaping your own blessings.

BE A BREAKER

Are you ready to take your place? Are you willing to do something about your storm? Can you honestly say, "God, I give it all to you, I want nothing else but to be a breaker for breakthrough by serving You with all of my heart, as meekly and as humbly as I can"? Ask Him for a fresh revelation of who you are and who He is, and seek to know Him. Don't wait for God to rebuke your unbelief, do something about it. Don't wait for someone else to do it for you either. How often do we run and ask someone else to pray for us before we even pray for ourselves? How often do we settle only on the teachings of others, rather than sitting at the Rabbi's feet and learning firsthand the principles of the Kingdom? What of your Kingdom character? Is it in the plumb line of the King's edict, does it line up with the Declaration of the Kingdom? Do you have the character of a Kingdom citizen?

Authority is in your hand, and if you're living by the Kingdom statutes, yours is the dominion and the authority to rule and reign with Christ Jesus as a joint heir. The duty is yours; the results are God's. What are you going to do about your mountain? Declare that it shall become a plain! Speak to poverty and say, "Enough is enough! Get out of my way!" You don't have to wait for the preacher to finish his sermon so he can lay hands on you for your sickness. Determine to take dominion and rise above that sickness. Stare that sickness down and see it in the spirit realm for what it is. See the cancer, see the heart condition, and say, "That's it! Be gone in the mighty name of Jesus Christ of Nazareth!"

Pray over another and say, "Silver and gold I have none, but what I do have I give you right now. I have authority over that sickness, and I say, 'Be gone! You will not cling to this person any longer.'" Rise up and rebuke every spirit of infirmity and every spirit of oppression and every spirit of witchcraft operating within your realm of authority. You are there, the glory is in you, the Kingdom is in you, and all of Heaven is going to back you up. Get the anointing for breakthrough. The Kingdom of Heaven suffers violence and the violent take it by force. Forcefully push your way into breakthrough, prophesy to your soul as David so often did: "Why are you cast down, O my soul? And why are you disquieted within me? Hope in God, for I shall yet praise

Him for the help of His countenance" (Ps. 42:5; see also Ps. 42:11; 43:5). Tell it, "I will rise up and hope in God! I will rebuke my storm. I take authority over it and command it to abate, to stop, to cease."

Every place you put the soles of your feet, you can advance the Kingdom. Every time you take a step, you advance the frontlines. Push back the resistance. Tell the devil, "Do you know who I am? I think it's time you knew. I also know that it's time that you know that I know who you are. Enough is enough! I am making a new decree that I am on the offensive from this day forward. I ain't running! The staff of authority is in my hand, and I stretch it forth right now. God is my partner and you lose!"

KINGDOM REINFORCEMENTS:

- Disobedience, attitudes of the heart, the flesh, unforgiveness, and dissention can hinder the amount of ground you can take for the Lord. Ask Him to reveal those issues. Pray for forgiveness.

- Close your eyes and think about what you carry. Decree your circumstances and take dominion over them with the power and authority God has already given you.

- Prophesy to your soul.

- Think about ways you can fill yourself up more with God and make plans to do so.

- We are what we behold. What do you behold? Spend time in your quiet place with God and share your dreams with Him. Maybe He'll give you new ones and point you to the stars in the sky as He did for Abraham.

Personal Prayer

Heavenly Father, I want to advance Your Kingdom, to partner with You and delegate with a true mantle of Kingdom authority and dominion. I ask You to forgive me for not advancing the territory with the Gospel as I should—for not taking more ground before now. I'm ready now. Impart in me a fresh, new revelation of who I am in You. Let the words and teachings I've learned nestle deep within my heart. Please open the eyes of my understanding and give me wisdom and revelation. Help me to hear Your voice in the thunder of the battle-grounds. I pray for that authority and dominion now, Lord. Please give me the robes of authority—train and strengthen my hands for war. Rise up and scatter my enemies. "Who are you, O mountain? You shall become a plain." I take authority over my circumstances, over the torment. I take authority in my city—my nation. Take me to the front lines now, God. Teach me to be a good steward of Your Kingdom. Help me to be a stargazer, Lord, to be focused on You, and to behold Your visions and destiny for me in Your Kingdom. Help me to become an expression of Your fullness and thank You for letting me partner with You. I'm here, God. Use me to advance the knowledge of Your glory over the earth, as the waters cover the sea. Amen.

ENDNOTES

1. David Guzik, "Commentary on Matthew 5," *David Guzik's Commentaries on the Bible* (Enduring Word Media, 1997-2003), http://www.studylight.org/com/guz/view.cgi?book=mt&chapter= 005 (accessed 13 November 2007).

2. Ibid.

CHAPTER 7

THE KING
AND THE PRIEST

Who are you when nobody is looking? Here are two biblical fellas who were who they were all of the time: Samuel (the priest) and David (the king). They had something very important in common. They both sought God's heart, and when God examined theirs, He found them to be true shepherd-type hearts that desired to know Him (and did know Him) intimately. God fulfilled their destinies because they positioned themselves before God and practiced His presence so that they could do what they saw the Father do and know His heart.

It's time for us to put away childish things, to mature, and to advance as kings and priests, wielding our God-given authority, just as He intended (see 1 Cor. 13:11). I hear a loud roaring in the heavenlies from the Lion of the Tribe of Judah, Jesus Christ. He's roaring against His enemies, pushing them back so that Christians will have greater freedom to rise up into their destinies as kings and priests in the Kingdom of God, "on earth as it is in Heaven."

Heavenly Father, we thank You for what You are opening before us by Your Spirit. Please give us the Spirit of wisdom and revelation and complete liberty in the Spirit so that we are free to enter into a deeper revelation concerning Your plans and purposes for the Body of Christ as kings and priests ruling in this world. Please help us always to become sponges, soaking up everything You want us to know and retain. In the name of Jesus, thank You!

THE LION OF THE TRIBE OF JUDAH ROARS

In the midnight hours one particular morning, I prayed, "God, I'm heading off to sleep now, but I want to awaken in the morning with a Holy Spirit download for my conference tonight. I want to receive revelation of its theme and its prophetic sense, as per Your will."

Exactly as my eyes closed for the night, I had a vision of Jesus Christ wearing a scarlet-blue kingly robe that represented His authority, His royalty, and His righteousness. I knew in my spirit that Jesus was clothed with great authority. I also saw a crown in His hand. As I looked at Him more closely, I realized He had the face of a lion, and in an instant, three revelations struck me as the Lion roared: that this Man was the Lion of the Tribe of Judah, that the vision of Him meant an increase in the level of authority, and that it was the kingly anointing. Hallelujah!

I believe that in this vision there were prophetic promises: that when the Lion of the Tribe of Judah roars there will come about an anointing for a release of the roar of the Lion in our spirits today.

1. The Roar Sets Captives Free

His roar sets captives free! Those who sit in darkness will come forth into freedom in Christ. Hosea prophesied that Ephraim (a symbol of a prodigal son or daughter) would walk after the Lord and follow His ways after the lion roars:

> *"How can I give you up, Ephraim? How can I hand you over, Israel? How can I make you like Admah? How can I set you like Zeboiim? My heart churns within Me; My sympathy is stirred. I will not execute the fierceness of My anger; I will not again destroy Ephraim. For I am God, and not man, the Holy One in your midst; and I will not come with terror. They shall walk after the Lord. He will roar like a lion. When He roars, then His sons shall come trembling from the west; they shall come trembling like a bird from Egypt, like a dove from the land of Assyria. And I will let them dwell in their houses," says the Lord* (Hosea 11:8-11).

When there is a release of the roar in Zion, not only is there a release of the captive sons and daughters, but also an actual planting of destiny as they come to dwell in the house of the Lord and root themselves firmly in Him. On behalf of the prodigals, I hear the Lion roar today. How would you like the Lion to roar over your family and shake the darkness loose? You can receive this today as a prophetic promise.

2. The Roar Pronounces Judgment Upon Our Enemies

Joel prophesied about a call of the nations to assemble in the

Valley of Jehoshaphat, where God would sit to judge all the surrounding nations. Then the prophet spoke about the Lord *roaring* from Zion against Israel's enemies, but he said that the Lord would be a shelter and strength for His people, the children of Israel (see Joel 3:11-12).

When the Lion roars, judgment will come against our enemies. Trust that we, God's people, will find shelter, but only if we walk in humility with complete devotion to the Lord. Ponder this as you study that third chapter of Joel.

3. *The Roar Stirs our Hearts for Spiritual Warfare*

Isaiah prophesied that the Lord would come down and fight for Mt. Zion and its hill:

> *For thus the Lord has spoken to me: "As a Lion roars, and a young lion over his prey (when a multitude of shepherds is summoned against him, he will not be afraid of their voice nor be disturbed by their noise), so the Lord of hosts will come down to fight for Mt. Zion and for its hill* (Isaiah 31:4).

This passage of Scripture speaks of aggression and stirs within us a response to the call for the mighty warriors to rise up. When a lion roars, the prey freezes with fear so that the lioness can go in and take the prey. The roar of the Lion of Judah will paralyze the enemy, causing fear and dread so that we, the Lioness (the Church and the Bride of Christ), can take our prey. The roar will release in our spirits an increase of authority so that we can engage in aggressive spiritual warfare that will immobilize the enemy's plans.

EXPERIENTIAL AND POSITIONAL TRUTHS

Isaiah prophesied of the never-ending Kingdom: "Of the increase of His government and peace there will be no end..." (Isa. 9:7a). He also said that the government of God rests upon His shoulders (see Isa. 9:6). God bears the burden of shouldering this immense responsibility of governing, but He invites us to co-labor with Him in the administration of His government in the earth, and He gives us a kingly, priestly anointing to carry this through.

The government of God is coming, and it's already happening, all at the same time. This means that *positional truth* (coming) is connecting to *experiential truth* (happening). Positional truth is receiving by faith the truth of the Bible—what God's Word says about us and about what we can do through the supernatural provision available to us—the "I can do all things through Christ who strengthens me" (see Phil. 4:13). Living that positional truth is acting on and growing in those things. However, positional truth and experiential truth work simultaneously. Thus the principle is that our destiny is already established in the Heavenlies (positional), but we each must contend for it and cooperate with God to bring it into existence in our everyday lives (experiential).

Isaiah connected the never-ending increase of God's government with the throne of David:

> ... *Upon the throne of David and over His kingdom, to order it and establish it with judgment and justice from that time forward, even forever. The zeal of the Lord of hosts will perform this* (Isaiah 9:7b).

So let's examine King David's life, particularly because he experienced many circumstances that are great examples of positional and experiential truths. Are you ready for a little wilderness training?

Truth #1: True Kings Receive Training in the Wilderness

God chose David to be the king of Israel when David was just a young man (see 1 Sam. 16:1-13). Samuel identified him as such when the Lord told him to go to the house of Jesse because He had selected one of the man's sons to reign as king over Israel. The prophet went as God directed him to, but when he surveyed the seven boys, although each of them could possibly be a contender for the role, they really didn't have the goods, and so the Lord eliminated each one. There was Samuel, wondering, and he asked the father if he had any more children. Imagine his relief to learn of the youngest one out tending the sheep. Immediately, as Samuel laid eyes on David, the Lord said, "Arise, anoint him; for this is the one" (1 Sam. 16:12). Here we see the positional truth in action as Samuel poured the oil upon David and anointed him as King of Israel—and note—long before he would experience the full manifestation of his kingship.

Do you see what we have here? Out of many brothers, out of many people, in fact, David had the favor of the Lord, and thus the Lord called him to the great task and position of king of Israel. The ministry of God came to him and consequently he became king: "The Spirit of the Lord came upon David from that day forward (1 Sam. 16:13).

Even though God had anointed him king through Samuel and

he had yet to see it come to fruition, David found himself thrust into several life and death situations (see 1 Sam. 17-19). He found favor with King Saul for a season, but it metamorphosed into a deadly disfavor that caused David to become an "outlaw." At times he had to run into the wilderness like a dog and even hide in the caves to escape Saul's pursuit of him.

Even though David had lost favor with the king, something amazing happened to him while in hiding. He gained the favor of 400 disgruntled, discontent outcasts who gathered to him and came to his side. These men were debtors and in distress, but they saw something in David that drew them to him—great character and leadership capabilities. They saw a bold warrior who, as a boy, single-handedly slew the giant Goliath, and they saw a young man who didn't retaliate when Saul tried to kill him. They knew a good leader when they saw one.

How many of us have heard great things about our destiny as King David did, but haven't seen something manifested in our lives? We've been told big stuff, had big dreams, seen great visions from our big God, but we've waited years for the fulfillment of them. Some of us are even in that wilderness place feeling like outlaws as we await the manifestation of our calling.

It could be that you're in training as David was in training. Adversity was having its perfect work, but David didn't rebel against adversity; instead, He proved himself as a true king, one trained in the wilderness of experiential truth. It could be that you are facing adversity, but it does have a perfect work in you, for God may be raising up a leader, and your actions may determine if you have the qualities it takes to be one.

Truth #2: Wilderness Brings Warfare

David's wilderness experience was rough. It would have been normal for him to think, *I don't look like a king…I don't feel like a king…what kind of kingdom is this anyhow?* Instead, he takes outcasts and misfits and trains their hands for war. Meanwhile, he had to have been thinking about how he would ever get from Point A to Point B, what with Saul and the whole army after him for several years.

Seek God Early

Imagine yourself in that situation. You've been told you are to be king, and yet the existing king and all of his minions are after you. You're forced to hole up in the wilderness, in damp, dark caves away from the comforts of family and home. It would be hard to hang on to the dream, wouldn't it? Instead though, David trained the hands of his followers for war, even though he couldn't see how it would all pan out. In Psalm 63, we see just how intense this wilderness warfare was for David. He cried out, "O God, You are my God; early will I seek You; my soul thirsts for You; my flesh longs for You in a dry and thirsty land where there is no water" (Ps. 63:1). David did exactly what he had to do in the wilderness. He sought God early, he thirsted for God's presence, and he didn't give up when all outward signs pointed to defeat.

When I learned that healing was a part of the Christian faith, I asked God for healing for my mother. Over and over I'd pray for her healing. However, this only fueled the fire for healing to work through me—it raged with a holy zeal and determination to see all the deaf hear! To that end, in every healing meeting I conducted, I'd ask for healing of the deaf and call them to the front altar. It was tough! In the early days, not one would hear, or someone might receive partial recovery. I had to believe for all—I couldn't give up or accept defeat. It was God's will that all would be healed, and I was determined to see it happen. Mark 9:25 refers to a demon called the "deaf and dumb spirit" which the Lord commanded to come out of a boy. I believe that, because I persisted, God gave me a revelation and breakthrough concerning this. Suddenly, I started to a see many more healed in my meetings when I cast out this spirit, particularly in Africa, where I'd say that about one out of every ten children who come to our meetings is deaf, mute, or deaf/mute. When Jesus cast out the demon afflicting the man with muteness, the mute man spoke (see Matt. 9:32-33).

Some people think that I am where I am in ministry because God just plunked me there. While this is certainly God's call on my life, I had to take action for breakthrough. As a brand new Christian, even in the first few months, I'd pray for hours and then go out and "do the stuff," over and over again. I'd go into the inner city streets of Vancouver, along the infamous "Hastings and Main" stretch of homeless people and drug dealers, pimps and prostitutes, or into the skateboard parks or the malls, to preach and demonstrate the Gospel. At first, it was slow, but then things picked up and I'd win 20 or 30 souls in an afternoon. There was another season when I'd spend almost every day in the park evangelizing and doing open air preaching. I ran a coffeehouse ministry from the basement of my small church for those on the streets, and if they didn't come, we'd go out and find them.

People sometimes wait for things to happen. I hear it all the time. "God has called me to preach, to move in miracles, signs, and wonders, but I'm just waiting for the power."

I say, "What are you waiting for? Why aren't you in the hospices? Why aren't you doing the stuff, contending, birthing, maturing, and nurturing what God's given you. You have authority; once you start exercising it, God will reward it. He always blesses us in our faithfulness to invest, multiply, contend, and pray, pressing in, even when things seem dry.

You might not see a hint of revival in your community or even your family. Someone you've been praying for may still be sick. Perhaps you're awaiting breakthrough for something personal but it doesn't look as though God is even planning to help. Nevertheless, although you're feeling parched, although things seem dry and bare with no sign of God, seek Him early, seek Him often, and not only with your heart, but with your whole being. Your flesh, all of your desire, should point to God. David didn't cry out, "O God, O God, You said I would be king—make me king!" No, he cried out for God Himself—the person of God, who God was, the very essence of God—to quench his thirst. In this psalm, David is making it clear that without God's presence it's as though he's dying. He's thirsty; he needs the water of life. That water is the Holy Spirit, the presence of God. The presence of God alone will drive out his enemies, so he cries out to God. Here's what that living water does: "I will open rivers in desolate heights, and fountains in the midst of the valleys; I will make the wilderness a pool of water, and the dry lands springs of water" (Isa. 41:18).

The devil hates water, and he'll leave us alone when we're wet with the Holy Spirit. Devils like the dry places, but the water flowing through desolate heights, streaming through the midst of valleys, pooling in the wilderness, and springing up in dry lands will drive them out.

Do you recall the story of the demoniac in the country of the Gadarenes that Jesus was about to cast out? The head demon, "Legion," begged Jesus not to cast them out of the country, but instead into a herd of 2,000 swine. Jesus acquiesced, they entered the swine, and the herd ran violently off a cliff and into the sea where they drowned (see Mark 5:1-13). Did Jesus allow this because He knew how much they hated water? I think yes! One day, demons will be in the lake of fire.

Truth #3: Grace in the Wilderness

Not only is Jesus an expert when it comes to dealing with demons, He provides for us in the wilderness when it's dry and there's no water: "I will even make a road in the wilderness and rivers in the desert" (Isa. 43:19). Rivers not only flow with water, but with grace. If we'll receive His grace, He'll pour it on us like a river of blessing, "Thus says the Lord: 'The people who survived the sword found grace in the wilderness—Israel, when I went to find give him rest'" (Jer. 31:2).

When we're in the wilderness, it may be tempting to rebel and just throw in the proverbial towel. God may come and make a grace offer, but it's like we just want out of there. "Thank You very much God!"—and we're off. However, check out David. His predicaments prove that he received the offer of grace and received a big dose of it. He fairly cried out to God, "I'm so hungry for You God! I'm hungry for Your glory. I'm hungry for Your power. I'm going to dig. I'm not going to let up or shut up. I have these 400 men, and we're going to war; we are not going to give up in this wilderness. It's dry, yes; I'm thirsty, yes; there's no water, yes;

I don't see a way out—but I'm not giving up. I accept Your grace—I welcome You!"

David persevered in the wilderness. This proved his character and mirrors what Paul the apostle taught when he said: "And not only that, but we also glory in tribulations, knowing that tribulation produces perseverance; and perseverance, character; and character, hope" (Rom. 5:3-4).

Character Pruning

When God saw David's character maturing steadily and producing great fruit, He decided to do some pruning: "...And every branch that bears fruit He prunes, that it may bear more fruit" (John 15:2b). After a long season of pruning—fighting, training his men, and running from Saul—David is led by the Lord to Hebron, where he is anointed king over the house of Judah, and then later he's anointed King over Israel (see 2 Samuel 2:1,4; 5:3).

It's in Hebron where David begins to experience more of the manifestation of the kingly anointing. It's as if God is saying, "I'm trusting you with more in this next season. Now you're going to go from the wilderness with trained men, rather than discontented bums and outcasts. You trained their hands for war! You were faithful. I am going to bring an increase of authority upon your life and it's going to intensify in Hebron."

KEEP CONTENDING FOR YOUR DESTINY

Hebron means "seat of association, friendship, society"[1] Today Hebron is called *el-Khulil* by the Muslims—which is what they call Abraham—meaning "the Friend," that is, of God.[2] Today, Hebron is a city struggling with a lot of spiritual warfare. Historically, when the 12 spies went into Canaan they eventually came into the Negev region, to Hebron, where the descendants of Anak lived: Ahiman, Sheshai, and Talmai, whose father was Anakim (see Num. 13:22). *Anak* means "to choke, strangle, and struggle with death." *Ahiman* means "to block or hinder." *Sheshai* means "to whiten or white wash." These sons were giants in the land.

After the children of Israel wandered in the wilderness for 40 years, when they finally came into their inheritance (under Joshua's leadership), Caleb asked for Hebron as his inheritance. Caleb said that with the Lord's help he would drive out the giants, the sons of Anakim. He did just that! (See Joshua 15:14.) Caleb was 85 years old then and as strong as an ox. Throughout the Scriptures, we see the children of Israel having to deal with demonic powers similar to the ones in Anakim's three sons.

Just as Caleb had his giants, just as David had his giants in Goliath and Saul, so too do we have giants that we have to overcome. We must persevere. We must press through. God will use every difficulty that comes our way as a way for us to build resistance—our spiritual muscles. When the enemy tries to choke us to death and hinder us from moving ahead—when he tries to whitewash everything so we just settle for less—we need to rise up and fight back with God's strategy. We need to contend for our destinies.

The enemy will try to whitewash—that is, obscure—our vision so that we don't see things as they really are.[3] He whitewashes us so that we'll settle for things the way we see them, taking on the attitude that it's simply life, or your lot in life, so grin and bear it. This also may lead us to complacency, whereby we just lay down and refuse to get involved for whatever reason. You know the scoop. It's a mindset that says something like, "Oh God, I want you to bless those hungry children," but then we turn the television channel to something else that's more palatable. We figure it's someone else's problem, or that it doesn't pertain to us, or doesn't affect us, and so shrug our shoulders and tune into something else.

Famine, war, poverty, the lost, the dying, cancer, infirmity, apathy—these things should make you rise up in spiritual violence! The violent take it by force (see Matt. 11:12). Why not set the standard? Why not press in? Why not get breakthrough? When things are hard and dry, worship and cry out to God even more. If things don't seem to be happening in your life, don't give up. If there's no manifesting, no oil, and no sense of God's presence, keep contending.

New as a Christian, I received a prophetic word that one day I'd preach to stadiums full of people just as Bill Graham does. Oh how this excited me—I thought, "Wow, cool! Stadiums for the Lord!" But I had to do my time. I preached on the streets in skid row, in sleazy coffee shops, in skateboard parks, in the inner city—preaching to prostitutes, drunks, and the down and out and the outcasts. It was far from the polished, shiny comfortable vision of stadium preaching! I had to get dirty, get into the ditches, and get way out of how I thought the vision should have unfolded. I had to do my time. I had to build resistance to the enemy. I had to show myself a leader to the outcasts.

Even as I went about doing this though, I didn't lose sight of the vision. God called me as an evangelist and gave me big dreams, so I did the time—four hours a day on the streets, three hours a day, at least, in His presence. He gave me another vision of *Fresh Fire* (my present ministry), and how it would grow and reach the world. Nevertheless, there I was, still on the streets of one city, but now pounding pavement and happy tapping for the Lord with my team.

True kings need wilderness time. The wilderness grew David into his position. God pruned him there and in Hebron so that he would produce maximum fruit for the Kingdom as king of Israel. David passed the test in the caves, and then God sent him to Hebron. There, he'd rise even higher as a trusted leader, contending for his kingly anointing.

God's continually pruning me. It's been an ongoing process of repentance and personal holiness, time invested in the secret place of His presence and in worship. So often, our own sins of bitterness, envy, pride, jealousy, or unforgiveness, hinder our usefulness. Sometimes we're too caught up being busy, and we skew our priorities. In the coming days, as we allow this pruning and testing, as we truly turn to the Lord, He will revive us, and He will raise us up, that we may live in His sight (see Hab. 6:1-2).

Just when I think I'm strong in faith, an obstacle comes into my life that seems to test it. It might be financial need, and God might even use it to test me. If I begin to doubt God or work out how I can save myself if He doesn't rescue me, He reminds me of the many times He's come through for me. As I remember His last-minute 11th-hour provision in the past, I cry out again, "God help!" and He comes through, just in time! Of course, I repent that I didn't believe God and ask His forgiveness. However, we have to understand that sometimes these tests of our faith are to strengthen our faith. He wants you ready to believe for Him to raise the dead. He wants us to think big like He does. As big as "Who are you, O great mountain?

Before Zerubbabel you shall become a plain!" (Zech. 4:7a). Walking in such faith for the seemingly impossible is to lay hold of spiritual substance in the heavenly realm and bring it into our natural realm. Listen, a few years ago now I had an extended time in the wilderness. What the Lord has done since is even more phenomenal in our ministry than it was before. I thought what the Lord had done through us in the earlier days was awesome and radical, but today, Fresh Fire Ministries is a global ministry leading even more thousands to Christ each year. We hold huge crusades and minister to people at home and abroad, shedding the love of God around the world for the glory of God and His Kingdom. God's principles and precepts for spiritual and personal growth worked for David, they worked for me, and they'll work for you.

PROMOTIONS INVITE DIFFICULTIES

When David emerged as an outstanding leader, God promoted him and sent him to Hebron where he was anointed King of Judah. However, there he experienced even more intense spiritual warfare, because Anak's descendants lived there. They created a nesting place for darkness. With the new level came new devils.

How would you like the kind of promotion that by its very nature just seems to invite great difficulties? Most of us would never sign up for hard times, but God knows that adversity builds both our character and our spiritual muscles. The psalmist expressed this so well: "I know, O Lord, that Your judgments are right, and that in faithfulness You have afflicted me" (Ps. 119:75). King David's promotion worked to his advantage because he gained great strength and wisdom in Hebron, overcoming many enemies both in the natural and spiritual realms (see 2 Sam. 2:5).

God didn't want David just to camp in Hebron for a few days. Rather, it was a necessary place to live so that he could grow in maturity for the next leg of his journey. God designed David's pilgrimage to include many difficulties, on purpose. He knew that adversity would prepare him to reign in the kingly anointing from Zion, the city of Jerusalem (see Ps. 84:5-7). David didn't get rebellious on this tough road. His heart attitude always wanted to please God, and this focus motivated him.

The Priestly Anointing is Foundational

King David eventually left Hebron and was anointed King over Israel, reigning from Jerusalem (see 2 Sam. 5:3-7). He walked in the kingly anointing. Consider that "David went on and became great, and the Lord God of hosts was with him" (2 Sam. 5:10). Before David ever became king, and although he wasn't part of the Levitical priesthood as Aaron (Moses' brother) and Zadok (the son of Ahitub) were, he possessed the heart of a priest. The function of a priest is very much like that of a pastor. Pastors are referred to as shepherds, so it's not surprising that David's heart (as a priest) would go hand-in-hand with his role as a shepherd.

He was a true protector over his family's flock of sheep—an excellent shepherd. He didn't flinch when it came to making sure each little sheep was safe. When a prowling lion or bear approached his flock, he put his life on the line and fought the intruders (see 1 Sam. 17:36). He was a hero when no one was watching. He wouldn't be featured in *People* magazine, nor would he receive a Nobel Prize, but God saw him from Heaven above as a proud Father watching His child. He knew that because David risked his life for the sheep when no one was looking, he'd do it when there were onlookers.

David had a passionate heart. He was a lover of God, one who desired deep intimacy with Him. When no one was around, David would take his stringed instrument and compose psalms and hymns to the Lord. He likely danced wildly in the pastures, too. God watches what we do in secret.

I know some people in ministry who put on that Sunday or ministry look with the air of, "I'm important to the Church—look at me!" Yet at home or in their daily lives, they might not pray all week. There are some preachers out there who only preach because it's their position—for no other reason than that. They don't spend time practicing the presence of God, seeking Him and His will for the message or the word that the Father has for them to preach. Instead, they pull out their prepared sermons that make them look good, polished, and worthy of their calling. Not. They don't have the heart of a priest or the heart of a shepherd because they don't really know the High Priest and the Shepherd.

TRUE PRIESTS ESTEEM GOD'S HOLINESS

When we have the heart of a faithful priest, we have the right foundation so that God can increase our level of authority and bring us into a kingly anointing. But make no bones about it—great responsibility accompanies the priestly anointing.

A Faithful Heart

The Lord spoke to Eli (the priest) concerning his two sons because they didn't have the faithful hearts required of a priest. In fact, they acted wickedly and despised the things of God to such a degree that God had to pronounce His judgment against them (see 1 Sam. 2:12-17,22,31-32). Nevertheless, God did show compassion to Eli when He said that He would raise up a faithful priest and anyone who was left in Eli's household would be permitted to approach him:

> Then I will raise up for Myself a faithful priest who shall do according to what is in My heart and in My mind. I will build him a sure house, and he shall walk before My anointed forever. And it shall come to pass that everyone who is left in your house will come and bow down to him for a piece of silver and a morsel of bread, and say, "Please, put me in one of the priestly positions, that I may eat a piece of bread" (1 Samuel 2:35-36).

A faithful priest in God's eyes is a servant who will do what is in His heart and mind. Now I want to ask a question. How can we do what's in God's heart and mind (only doing those things that we see the Father doing) if we don't take the time to see what the Father's doing? (See John 5:19.) We have to seek the heart and mind of God. Drop the personal agendas. Forget trying to look the part. Seek the mind of Christ, His agenda, and be sensitive to it.

Eli functioned as a priest during the days when the word of the Lord was rare and visions were infrequent (see 1 Sam. 3:1). His eyes were so dim that he couldn't see—a mirror of his spiritual condition. Thus, the boy Samuel (who was in Eli's care) ministered to the Lord and the word of the Lord began to come to him. "Samuel. Samuel. Samuel!" It took God calling the boy's name three times before Eli's prophetic sensitivity kicked in that perhaps the voice calling young Samuel belonged to God (see 1 Sam. 3:4-8).

After his many years spent walking in God's presence, what happened to Eli? I believe that He neglected to lie down where God's presence was, and this resulted in Eli's household having no regard for God's holiness. The true priestly anointing always reflects the holiness of God. God's presence nourishes that.

Judgment Begins at the House of God

Eli's sons didn't resist temptation, and Eli failed to rebuke them. His sons lay with the women who served at the doorway of the tent of meeting. Eli knew, but he did nothing (see 1 Sam. 2:22; 3:13). However, God knew and He was going to do something, for the Father will not be mocked (see Gal. 6:7). He has a standard of righteousness and a divine plumb line that we're to heed (see Amos 7:7-8; Zech. 4:10).

God is examining many people in ministry today because it's judgment time concerning the House of God. Woe to the pastor or preacher who hasn't confronted today's controversial, sensitive, or pressing issues in his or her church or ministry. For the sake of political correctness, for financial support, or for the fear of rejection, many haven't wanted to "rock the boat."

Hear this though—in these days, God is looking for those who will call sin what it is, for those who will preach the message of the

Gospel that exposes, convicts, and leads to repentance. He searches for those who will take responsibility to speak up, for those who will violently rock that dead-on-the-water boat until it keels over, dumps out, and exposes all of that impurity, including apathy and complacency. Eli's attitude was, "Oh, I don't want to get my hands dirty as far as my boys are concerned—what they do is their business." That wasn't the case, was it? God called a great famine upon Eli in the form of the rarity of God's audible voice.

Of course, we always do these things in love and in wisdom (see Eph. 4:15), but if something's going on in your ministry or your church (if you're the pastor or an elder), then you have a responsibility to speak up. If you know of something going on in your home church or a ministry you attend, share it with the leader. For the leader, the responsibility is to speak up, and only then can the leader be absolved of the responsibility. Don't be like Eli, doing nothing about immorality, prayerlessness, worldliness, apathy, love without action or passion—these types of things must be addressed.

God did come to Eli, but He judged his house. The apostle Peter spoke about God's judgment coming first to the household of God: "For the time has come for judgment to begin at the house of God; and if it begins with us first, what will be the end of those who do not obey the gospel of God? (1 Pet. 4:17).

God removed the priestly mantle from Eli and his household. In effect He told Eli, "You're not going to be in My house anymore, for I am about to raise up a faithful priest, one who will do what's in My heart and what's on My mind."

Young Samuel was whom God chose to raise up because He saw the boy's heart and He knew Samuel would do His will. Samuel became God's trusted prophet, a man who grieved over sin and one who had the authority to anoint David as king (see 1 Sam. 16:1). Hallelujah! Do you see? Does it all tie in for you now, this kingly/priestly anointing? Do you see how it all connects? Samuel spoke prophetic wisdom because he knew God's heart. This is all to bring us to the following: we cannot move into the kingly anointing without the prophetic anointing, and we cannot move into the prophetic anointing without the priestly anointing that also comprises the shepherd anointing.

Now you might say, "Yes, David devoted his heart to the Lord, but he wasn't without sin. In fact, he was involved in a great sin while living in Jerusalem. Why didn't God remove his anointing as He removed Eli's?"

The difference was that Eli didn't repent. David did. Because of David's repentance for his adultery, God wasn't forced (because of the Law) to remove the kingly anointing, but David did suffer God-ordained consequences because of what he did: "Now therefore, the sword shall never depart from your house, because you have despised Me, and have taken the wife of Uriah the Hittite to be your wife" (2 Sam. 12:10-11). Remember, you don't want to make mockery of God. We as Christians are accountable for our actions, and Christian leaders even more so, because they have influence with people and are supposed to set a standard for people to follow—raising the bar, so to speak.

KINGLY ANOINTING RELEASES CORPORATE ANOINTING

We prove that we have the heart of a faithful priest when we esteem the holiness of God, and when we are only concerned with doing God's will. Then we'll have what it takes to carry the kingly anointing. The kingly anointing involves a wide scope of spiritual authority because it releases a corporate anointing to see mass salvation, healing, or deliverances. For example, if a thousand demon-possessed people answered an altar call and accepted salvation, and then we prayed in the name of Jesus for all to be delivered *en masse,* that would be the carrying of a kingly anointing that releases a corporate anointing. Powerful, yes?

The corporate anointing may also be released upon other believers in an assembly to affect even more miracles and release considerable supernatural power to destroy the works of the enemy. When a group of believers minister healing together in the name of Jesus Christ of Nazareth, using the authority given, the result can be mass miracles that bring the Lord much glory. This corporate anointing may exceed what one believer can do.

God wants to release a new focus and new level of authority in the Body of Christ to advance His Kingdom. I see this new level in our ministry here at Fresh Fire where He is leading us to pray for thousands at one time in our crusades, commanding specific diseases to leave.

We're seeing mass results and it's awesome! During many of our miracle festivals, God not only saves and heals thousands, but He often sets many free from demonic bondages. We've seen some bound by evil spirits and insane, like the demoniac in the Gospels, set free by God's power. We've also seen up to a hundred or more demonized people set free at once. At times I've actually been led to take authority over a spirit of witchcraft, or another ruling spirit in the area, that was hindering God's work—the result was thousands coming to Jesus, being set free, and miraculously healed.

As I often emphasize, it's not about just one person on stage ministering. It's about a team walking in the power and love of Jesus. I remember the last night of our trip to Ongole, India. Of the crowd of 120,000 that flowed out into the streets (a record number at that time for an FFM meeting), 85,000 responded to the altar call for salvation, and there were hundreds more miracles reported. The people were so hungry they would literally fight to get through the crowd to receive prayer from a FFM team member.

Listen, time is short, and we don't all have four hours to cast out one devil. The Church needs such a level of authority and power to see entire stadiums full of people healed before they leave the stadium grounds. What a level of anointing this could be! But you have to esteem God's holiness. You have to survive the wilderness and learn resistance. You have to call on God early. You have to spend time letting Him fill you with the river of His presence. The priestly anointing, the kingly anointing, and the corporate anointing are only possible by being sold out to God, by being an active Kingdom disciple pressing in by force because of God's manifest presence and strength in you to do just that.

Can you imagine the kingly anointing operating in every believer to release a corporate anointing for cities, regions, and entire nations? There's an increase happening this very hour. It may seem cliché, but it's the hour of power.

God will use believers in various ways according to the level of authority they've been given. Some will affect a neighborhood, others a city, another Hollywood, another the government, and so on, but all of us must prepare our hearts to receive a whole lot more from God and never settle for anything less than all He has for us. It's the difference between life and death for the multitudes, many of whom will not enter the Kingdom of God if we don't forcefully press in.

WHAT'S GOD'S TESTIMONY OF YOU?

So, what have you learned thus far while we've examined significant clips from the lives of King David and Samuel, the king and the priest? Each of their lives comprises excellent examples of what it takes to please God and how to walk as kings and priests in this life.

Your heart must be sold out to God so that He can strongly support you as He supported those two men. "For the eyes of the Lord move to and fro throughout the earth that He may strongly support those whose heart is completely His" (2 Chron. 16:9 NASB).

What's God's testimony going to be of you? Of David, He said that David was a man after His own heart who would do His will (see Acts 13:22). Daniel sought God's presence and soaked in it, and the Bible records that the Lord was with him and let none of his words fail. Of Samuel, we know that God said to Eli that He would raise up for Himself "a faithful priest who will do according to what is in My heart and in My soul..." (1 Sam. 2:35). He built Samuel an "enduring house" (2 Sam. 7:14). All of Israel knew that Samuel was confirmed as a prophet of the Lord, and the Lord appeared again... and the Lord *revealed Himself* to Samuel..." (1 Sam. 3:21).

Glory! That's what I want, the Lord to appear again and again and again and reveal Himself to me. I want an enduring house, and you know you want it too.

TENDING THE TEMPLE LAMPS

How do you take care of the temple lamp stand? Do you burn on it the sweet incense of prayer every morning when you tend the lamps? (See Exodus 30:7-8.) Prayer makes the ground of your heart fertile so that you will hear and receive revelation. God wants to take you to a new level of intimacy, modeling Samuel's soaking and seeking, because that's the only way to go deeper. God is calling you—will it take three times or once for you to hear His voice? Pride, busyness, complacency, apathy, compromise—those things will all deafen your ears to the words of the High Priest. Are you ready for the roar of the Lion of Judah? Are you sure that you won't be swept into judgment with your enemies? Are you positioned for the roar that will see bondages broken and freedom come to your sons and daughters?

If you sense even a draft in your heart or feel a callused lump, burn sweet incense, lay before the Lord and minister unto Him, and ask Him to renew your passion for Him. All desire comes from Him.

The priestly and kingly anointings are your heritage. Live in the fullness of your heritage as a king and as a priest for the glory of the Kingdom. Are you willing to go through wilderness training, and are you able to get through it by receiving grace in the wilderness?

PERSONAL PRAYER

Dear Father, I want to grow into a new level of intimacy

with You. I want to go deep—deeper in You—and ask You to examine my heart, because I want to be a testimony to Your righteousness as Samuel was. Forgive me if there has been any complacency, any apathy, any callousness of my heart. Soften it, Lord. Release the roar of the Lion of the Tribe of Judah. Release that authority in my spirit, Lord. Take me into Zion, Lord, past the caves, the wilderness, and the giants in the land. Let the Spirit of Your word fall upon me in the deep, secret places of my heart. Fill me with the sweet, fragrant oil of Your Spirit and let me be a burning light of revival in the land. Pull me into the destiny of desire You have placed in my heart. I will press in, for I know that as the Lion roars, the giants will scatter. I take my position, Lord, with You in heavenly places over my obstacles. I'm hungry for what I see, God. What's my next step? Lord, I'm willing to war for my destiny—to keep the lamp fires burning and to draw closer toward the throne room. Pour Your anointing oil forth, as it did from Samuel's horn to King David.

Lord, there's been a famine of Your Word in my life. Father, forgive me for allowing my relationship with You to become stale. Forgive me for my prayerlessness and for not having a heart that waits on You. Lord, please release that Samuel anointing on my life today. I want to be a priest, to rest in the glory, and to know Your voice. I want to see what You are doing in Heaven, so I pray for the Spirit of wisdom and revelation. Let my heart be open to receive the word of the Lord, the prophetic word, the proceeding word, the healing word, and the word of knowledge. I want a download of the Spirit of prophecy. Please give me eyes to see and ears to hear so that I can understand those things You've planned in eternity. Father, I receive the Spirit of wisdom, revelation, counsel, and might. Let me be one of Your prophetic people. Lord, give me the word of knowledge for my workplace, for my school. Help me go into the marketplace as Your priest with Your anointing, authority, and mantle. Let me hear the word of the Lord, wherever I am. I thank You that today, just as in Samuel's day, out of true priesthood, You want to release a king. I believe that as You empower me to walk in those priestly and prophetic anointings, You will raise me up to kingly authority. Amen.

KINGDOM APPLICATIONS

- Contend for your destiny through the example of King David, with a heart sold out for God.

- Recognize the giants that come to steal your anointing.

- Study again why God chose to anoint David as king and Samuel as priest, and learn how to apply those principles to your life.

- Remember and revisit dreams, visions, and the

closeness you had with God when you first knew Him, and yearn for those things again. Remember where you were, the position you took, and take that position again. Get into the birthing position to receive all that God has for you.

- Grow in favor with God. Develop a priestly heart. Minister unto the Lord as Samuel did. Soak and seek. Keep the lampfires burning; grow in intimacy with Him. Burn incense, learn what it is to pray in the morning before you start your day. Value the heart of a priest.

- Understand the value of having a heart sold out for God, the heart of a priest.

⤙ CORPORATE PRAYER

Heavenly Father, we come to You today mindful that we need to surrender our lives to You completely. We want You to take us on the journey that You have tailor-made for us so that we can rise up into our kingly anointing. Please help us not to run away or refuse to allow You to have Your way with us. We want to say "Yes" to being led by You into the wilderness and the difficult places so that adversity can have its perfect work in our lives. God, please help us to contend for our God-ordained destinies by overcoming the enemy. Father, please help us to be as faithful priests concerning our prayer life and taking time to be with you. We want to walk in humility with devoted hearts, and we know that as we experience a deepening relationship with You, our hearts won't be callused or cold. We want to be diligent and faithful concerning Your Kingdom when no one is watching us. We want the kind of heart that pleases You, a heart that's only concerned with what's on Your heart and mind, God. Please anoint us with increased authority in our lives and the excitement of the kingly oil and the kingly dominion, the increase of Your government, Your rule, and reign. We need a whole new level of authority that will impact the masses. Father, please release Your heart and Your strategy so that cities, regions, and nations hear the good news of our Lord and Savior Jesus Christ. Thank you, God. Amen.

ENDNOTES

1. Roswell D. Hitchcock, *An Interpreting Dictionary of Scripture Proper Names* (New York, 1874), s.v. "Hebron," http://www.studylight.org/dic/hbn/view.cgi?number=T1054 (accessed 26 June 2008).

2. Dr. William Smith, *Smith's Bible Dictionary* (1901), s.v. "He'bron," http://www.studylight.org/dic/sbd/view.cgi?number =T1913 (accessed 26 June 2008).

3. See Matthew 23:27. Consider, ponder the Pharisees and the white-washed tombs.

CHAPTER 8

THE WAR ANOINTING

For we do not wrestle against flesh and blood, but against principalities, against powers, against the rulers of the darkness of this age, against spiritual hosts of wickedness in the heavenly places (Ephesians 6:12).

While the world is at odds and leaders busy themselves with strategies to fight physical wars, it should come as no surprise to God's people that we are engaged in a great spiritual battle. From the early chapters of the Old Testament in the Garden of Eden to the very last chapter of the New Testament, it is apparent that satan is the enemy of God and that he actively seeks to oppose God, His purposes, and His people. Satan has ravaged the world for many centuries, and his appetite for power is growing steadily as he seeks to deploy indirect methods to attack and destroy God's people. Alarmingly, countless believers today are easy prey. Many are apathetic. Some do not understand the devil's schemes, his weapons, or his tactics, nor do they know of the weapons, plans, and blueprints God has provided for their defense.

Nevertheless, the reality is that we're in battle. We're being prevailed against. Some of us are "losing" in the fight against sin and sickness, disease and death. Some of us are losing the battle for our kids to know Jesus. Some of us are battling for our marriages. Some of us are battling against poverty and the very things that hinder the fulfillment of the prophetic word in our lives. War wages for the fulfillment of our very divine destinies. The "one" we battle against is the very one who can keep a believer from achieving this goal.

As soon as we become blood-bought believers in the Lord Jesus Christ, we're thrust behind enemy lines, though assured of God's protection. However, we're also reminded that we operate in an environment of spiritual terrorism: "We know that we are of God, and the whole world lies under the sway of the wicked one" (1 John 5:19). Thus, we must recognize this and commit ourselves to train and be ready for battle, and even more so, in these last days, for unconventional spiritual warfare. Whether you are a marine fighting in the streets of Baghdad, a parent living in a sleepy suburb, or even the President of the United States, you must assume your position as a mighty spiritual warrior similar to that of an ancient soldier defending an empire (see Eph. 6:10-18).

We are at war. The closer we are to God, the more the enemy (satan) wants to separate and weaken us. This war has raged for centuries. The prophet Daniel saw the war we would face today: "I was watching; and the same horn was making war against the saints, and prevailing against them" (Dan. 7:21). This war is with the antichrist and the anti-anointing spirit. We're reminded in Daniel 10 about the Prince of Persia opposing Michael, the archangel, for 21 days. As the enemy opposed him, so the anti-anointing and anti-christ spirits oppose our very destiny and inheritance in God.

A Vision of God's Army

The Lord gave me a vision of His army—the army of the Lord, mighty warriors glowing with His radiance. I believe this army represented the Body of Christ today, particularly in North America. It's an army; yes, an army that God has called. However, I don't believe the army of the Lord that He showed me was as He had called it to be.

I knew this battlefield spoke of the spiritual battle we wage with demonic powers and principalities. I saw some mighty warriors wandering around in a daze, not knowing where they were. They groped about in the darkness as though unaware of their surroundings. The Holy Spirit revealed that many of the warriors didn't even realize they were in battle or treading in a combat zone. Some believed there was no battle and others did not believe they wrestled "not against flesh and blood, but against demonic powers and principalities."

They were blind to spiritual warfare and to their adversary, the devil—oblivious to the enemy's assignment on their lives. They were unaware that they'd even been drafted into God's army. However, whether they liked it (or believed it) or not, there was a battle and they were engaged in it.

Second Vision

In a second vision, I saw mighty warriors once again in the army of the Lord. They were children of light, girded in His armor. They shone with the light of God's glory and seemed completely at ease. Some casually ate sandwiches while resting against logs, and others just lazed on the grass and stared at the sky. Others fellowshipped with each other, yet all around them an intense battle raged. Weapons were within reach all over the place; I even saw weapons on the ground close to the warrior's feet, but they ignored them. The Holy Spirit revealed that this was the apathy of the army of the Lord.

Then birds flew out of the heavens, and they relentlessly assaulted and pecked at these casually laid-back and indifferent warriors. The Bible says that the birds of the air come to snatch away the Word of God (see Luke 5:5-15). The birds of the air are the demons that snatch away the Word from a man's heart, but only because a man leaves it out there, unprotected. The devil cannot take away the Word from our hearts if we hold it close and protect it. Only if we care nothing about it, then indeed, can the enemy snatch it from our hearts.

It seemed, though, that these soldiers considered the birds to be more of a nuisance than a threat. They complained and murmured, but not one on the battlefield reached for the sword of the Spirit to battle or protect themselves. The Lord spoke of the apathy of the army of the Lord (given the weapons of our warfare, given the reality of the armor of God, and given the victory through the shed blood of Jesus). Apathy kept them from using the weapons provided by the Holy Spirit.

We must be aware that we are on the front lines because there is a battle. Whether or not we believe in hell, there is one. Whether or not we believe in demons, the reality is that the enemy is real, as is spiritual warfare. We must wrestle against the demonic powers and principalities and take authority to bring them under our feet. Now is not the time for complacency. We must motivate ourselves to use and wield the weapons at our disposal and shed indifference or apathy. We must open our eyes to the seriousness of the threat of the enemy. In truth, many automatically assume they've won, when in reality they are defeated.

WAKE UP!

God is saying:

> *Proclaim this among the nations: "Prepare for war! Wake up the mighty men, let all the men of war draw near, let them come up. Beat your plowshares into swords and your pruning hooks into spears; let the weak say, 'I am strong.'" Assemble and come, all you nations, and gather together all around. Cause Your mighty ones to go down there, O Lord* (Joel 3:9-11).

Arise, take your plowshares, and wield them as swords. It is time to anoint the shield for the spiritual battle that is reality everyday, for everyday is a combat zone. Our warfare is against real demonic powers and principalities and a devil seeking to devour, kill, steal, and destroy. The Word of the Lord is to "be sober and alert."

These soldiers in my vision were mighty men and yet they were unmindful of the war that raged around them. Even those warriors in the vision who couldn't see the battle were mighty men.

Romans 13:11 says it's the hour to awaken, it's high time to awake out of sleep. The Bible says it was "time to awaken them for they slept."

RUN THE WALL

God wants to awaken you for battle. It's time to declare war, in Jesus' name. Are you ready to join the ranks of God's army? Wake up—arise! God looks for mighty warriors as described in Joel 2:

> *They run like mighty men, they climb the wall like men of war; every one marches in formation, and they do not break ranks. They do not push one another; every one marches in his own column. Though they lunge between the weapons, they are not cut down. They run to and fro in the city, they run on the wall; they climb into the houses, they enter at the windows like a thief* (Joel 2:7-9).

Will you enlist, run, and climb the wall? The wall is intercession, and God speaks to the wall's watchmen: "Take up My prophetic arrows." All of God's army, His saints, shall run and climb the wall. I believe God is releasing us into fervent prayer and intercession.

WIELD YOUR WEAPONS

Are you victorious in some areas but not in others? Do you shrink back or lunge between the weapons? There are reasons why we aren't overcoming certain battles, victories we should experience because of Jesus. We're to be mighty men and women who lunge between weapons. We are to engage in warfare and position ourselves in the front lines of the enemy's camp, even though we know it's going to cost us and that the battle may be fierce. A particular mindset in the Body of Christ today reasons, "If I don't touch, chase, or confront the devil or demon, I won't have to worry." Saints are afraid to become involved in spiritual warfare or take on a demon or the devil.

We must take up the sword of the Lord and fight the good fight of faith through the deployment of readily available weapons of our warfare. We can't lunge between weapons if we don't pick them up. We can't win the battles with weapons just laying there. When was the last time you used the weapon of the power of the blood of Jesus or wielded the power of Jesus' name, employed fasting and prayer, or lifted your shield of faith? Do you truly believe in them, in their power to overcome the enemy? If you're not using weaponry because you don't understand how to use them or what they are for, then it's important to learn. Seek a revelation of the power that is in the name of Jesus—the power of the Blood, the power of prayer and fasting, the power of the shield of faith, and then deploy those things. Often we forget what is available, but making these spiritual weapons a part of our lifestyle ensures that won't happen. Fast and pray, wield the name of Jesus, and lift high your shield of faith in every circumstance.

Shield of Faith

The shield of faith is our truth and our buckler. It's the truth of the Word of God, and it's given to every believer to quench the fiery darts of the wicked one (see Eph. 6:16). But it has to be used. We are to be *doers* of God's Word. When we act, the shield moves when we do, even if we don't even feel it there. Is your shield moving, or is it stationary? You must have God's Word to act on or else the enemy will get you in the back, so ingest the Word of God and feed on it regularly.

Other Weapons

Some spiritual weapons we forget are even there. We have a full armor of weaponry. There's the helmet of salvation, the breastplate of righteousness, belt of truth, the shoes of the gospel of peace, the sword of the Spirit, and prayer (see Eph. 6:10-20). Some of us put them on but don't deploy them. We don't really have the sword of the Spirit until we preach and proclaim what the Word of God says. We don't have the shield of faith until we walk in that faith. It's time to take up the armor of God. After all, we are mighty warriors! Our job is to lunge between the weapons. We are to not only climb the wall and intercede, but we are to run along it and become fervent in our intercessory warfare. When we proclaim God's Word instead of our feelings, circumstances, and symptoms, we are wielding the sword of the Spirit. Make this the year, the time, the moment that you take up the armor of God, wield the sword of the Spirit, and fight to win.

> *Oh Lord. Train our hands for war! Give us the anointing of the Lion of the Tribe of Judah. Let the Lion roar into the Heavenlies and into our spirits. Thank You, Lord, for the war anointing. Thank You for drafting us into Your army. Thank You for the fresh revelation of the weapons*

of our warfare. Thank You Lord, oh Spirit of God, for training and equipping our hands not just for war but also for the victory that we have in Jesus. Thanks be to God who always causes us to triumph in the name of Jesus.

God is sounding the alarm and calling the army of God to stand at attention. It is a critical hour for the Body of Christ to rise and lay hold of its inheritances. While very real wars rage on the earth, real war rages in the heavens. Plead for spiritual victory in your household. Prepare for victory in your finances, in your health, in your ministry. Ask for a harvest of souls and salvation, healing and deliverance. Look to Him for victory in your church and your city. Thank Him for causing you to triumph. Thank Him for releasing victory and war inside your spirit, that you and your loved ones might forever be transformed through war, victory, and prophetic intercession. The battle is yours to win. The increase of the Kingdom depends on it.

PERSONAL PRAYER

Heavenly Father, I'm sorry for my apathy and complacency, for letting the weapons of warfare—with which I am to take the Kingdom by force—lay on the ground unused. Father, I know that real war rages in the heavens, opposing Your will on earth, but I want to look to You for victory in my life, for my sons and daughters, for my church and my neighborhood. Please release war and victory in my spirit. I want to increase the Kingdom, and

I cannot do it without employing Your weapons that You've made readily available to me. Help me to be sure of who I am in You, as Your child, with the war anointing and the authority to wield and employ those weapons. Forgive me for sleeping. Awaken all of my senses as I draw close to You and prepare for battle. Awaken the warrior in me. Gird me with Your truth. By Your counsel and Your might, I'm ready to launch the grenades of Your dynamite Word. I love You Father. In Jesus' Name I pray, amen.

CHAPTER 9

CROWN OF FAVOR

We live in the most exciting age of all time. We are closer now to experiencing the greatest spiritual harvest since Pentecost. This is the hour of God's favor. It is the season of holy commissioning, destiny, empowering, and sending—the day of a mighty move of the Holy Spirit without measure.

The dew of the Lord is coming down, and when it lifts, there will be manna and lots of it. God is releasing showers of blessings on His chosen saints. We're talking *dunamis* power, the reality of Mark 11:23; 16:18, Acts 2:17-20, and Revelation 11:6. We will see ordinary men, women, and children move in signs and wonders. We'll see believers doing the great and greater works of John 14:12. I believe the day is coming when, through us, God will show signs and wonders in the heavens and the earth, when we will have the same power as Jesus had over the natural elements when the wind and the sea obeyed Him. I believe we will move into a ministry of wonders fulfilling Joel 2:30-31. We will speak to limbs as Jesus did in Luke 6:10 and see them made whole. We'll walk in authority as Joshua, who spoke and the sun stood still (see Josh. 10:12-13). We'll see the glory cloud literally come down upon the Church and see even children preaching with fire and boldness. Yes, I've seen great moves of healing and miracles by the hands of children and a prophetic Samuel generation in visions.

The former rain and latter rain have converged for the harvest. The dew of Heaven is resting on the seeds—seeds that have been on your heart, the seeds of destiny that have fallen upon dry ground. The dew, the latter, and the spring rains are coming. The seeds are budding, and soon they will yield much fruit.

The Day of Manifestation

Many have walked faithfully in the Spirit but haven't come into the day of increase, favor, and authority. But this day is coming as it did for Jesus and many great biblical saints. Scripture says that Jesus *increased* and kept *increasing* "in wisdom and stature, and in favor with God and men" (Luke 2:52).

John the Baptist, the son of Zacharias and Elisabeth, *grew* in wisdom, knowledge, and fortitude in his soul and was in the deserts "till the *day of his manifestation* (the day he commenced his ministry and declared his commission as Messiah's forerunner) to Israel" (Luke 1:80).

God's favor increased over King David. The Spirit of God came upon him when he was appointed king over Judah (see 1 Sam. 16:13). However, it took years before his kingship manifested—when he actually ruled and reigned over all of Israel. David received more measures of favor and authority when he reigned as king and even more as he grew as king. Every stage of his faithful, intimate walk with the Lord manifested more favor.

The fullness of the Spirit of God comes upon us when we accept Jesus into our hearts, and He gives us that initial measure of gifts and Holy Spirit power. However, these measures of gifts and blessings also increase as we seek to increase in favor with God.

The Spirit of the Lord says that God is placing a crown of manifestation on the heads of His faithful, diligent, chosen saints—a crown of great favor and authority with God and men, a new and greater installment of the fruits and blessings of the Spirit. Another measure, and another, and another. God rewards those who diligently seek Him (see Heb. 11:5). To those He calls His friends, He gives greater measures of authority and favor.

A Season of Birth

Favor is God's "pleasure." When God takes pleasure or delights in people, He distinguishes them, showering down His spiritual blessing, goodwill, and grace. He wants to bestow on us His unsearchable riches, and He enriches us with all spiritual blessings in faith and with the riches of grace and of glory, with no sorrow accompanying them.

We have entered into a time of increased favor, when God will empower and commission believers for harvest with greater authority, grace, spiritual blessing, faith, and supernatural provision. It is a season of birth—a season when His saints step into the fullness of His grace and birth great fruit, a season when God births and releases ministries and destinies.

GOD'S FAVOR QUALIFIES US

The fruit we bear glorifies God, and He says that He will anoint His diligent saints with an even greater manifestation of spiritual riches. He will favor the faithful with His riches. "The blessing of the Lord, it maketh rich, and He addeth no sorrow with it" (Prov. 10:22 KJV). He will literally *pour* His blessings upon the hands of the diligent (see Prov. 10:4). They will receive a new installment, an anointing of *incredible* depths of spiritual riches. His favor will cause them success. They will be the head and not the tail because of the favor He will pour over them. Experience won't be necessary because they'll have His favor, which empowers and therefore qualifies them to accomplish great feats.

God is commissioning His saints, upon whom His favor rests, with grace to do the impossible. God's glory will fall upon those in whom God delights.

THE SEASON OF CHOOSING

Moses placed Aaron's rod before the ark and it miraculously blossomed and bore almonds, a symbol of God's favor in choosing Aaron as high priest. In the culture of the Israelites, the rod symbolized authority. It was a tool used by the shepherd to correct and guide his flock (see Ps. 23:4). Both Aaron's and Moses' rods were symbols of authority and were endowed with miraculous power. With Moses' rod, God parted the Red Sea and brought forth water from a stone. God used Aaron's rod in his dealings with stubborn Pharaoh.

This is the season of choosing. God is placing the rod of kingship, favor, and authority in the hand of the chosen, and it's going to bud, man! It's going to blossom; it's going to bear fruit!

God wants to favor you. Consider Esther. He gave her everything she needed to receive the favor He desired for her. God gave her favor with Hegai who provided what she needed and advanced her to the best place in the king's harem (see Esther 2). This was a supernatural provision of grace.

Years ago, in an encounter, the Holy Spirit spoke to me and told me that I was one of many first fruits "sons and daughters" that would birth a ministry in a day. It was that quick. God's favor was upon me because I sought Him with all of my heart. I pursued Him and prepared myself to be chosen. So too, the Lord is choosing; and upon His chosen He is giving authority, power, and favor. Doors will swing open as God supernaturally provides in this day of manifestation.

You must have the *grace* to receive His favor. The Lord has told me that there is a seed time and a harvest time. There is a time to sow and a time to reap (see Eccles. 3:1-2). There's a time to labor in intercession as Elijah did, and then there's manifestation!

What Do You Wish?

There are seasons in which God *ordains seed time* and seasons where God ordains harvest. There are times to cast your bread upon the water and times it multiplies back to you. This is the season of multiplication, of manifestation, of God giving you what you desire. Even if you've asked a hundred times for one thing, in the season of favor, the heavens open and He grants what you ask of Him. Esther prepared and positioned herself to be pleasing before the king. So pleased was he, that he held out a golden scepter to her signifying His favor and an invitation into the palace. The king asked her, "What do you wish?" (See Esther 5:2-3.) This is the day that God selects those pleasing to Him and asks, "What do you wish?"

TIME IN THE TABERNACLE

Favor depends on friendship. Through intimacy, the Lord calls us His "friends" (see John 15:15). In friendship with Him, we are no longer servants. When we abide in Him, we can ask anything we desire, and it will be granted to us (see John 15:7). Favor depends on preparing ourselves and positioning ourselves to be pleasing before the King. It's time in the tabernacle, in the tent of meeting, meeting with God, worshiping, and spending intimate time with Him. It moves God when we prepare, and it delights Him to respond to our desires. Hosts of angels await the Lord's command in Heaven to release and manifest His blessings.

THE TENT OF WITNESS

In a vision, the Lord showed me the budding rod. An angel placed it in my hand, and God said, "I want to show them whom I have chosen." God will witness the call on your life. Those in the tent of meeting will move into the tent of witness.

In the tent of witness, God releases authority, influence, and favor. When Moses placed the 12 rods of the Father's houses in the tent of witness, Aaron's rod sprouted, put forth buds, blossomed, and yielded ripe almonds, while the rods of the rest of the princes remained dry and void of fruit. God bestowed a great deal of honor upon Aaron, anointing him high priest and providing him with an abundance of authority and blessings, all by reason of favor.

Because of His favor, you will receive a holy commissioning backed by Heaven, backed by God, and in the fullness of your calling breakthrough will manifest.

Who Does God Say You Are?

You will become a man or woman approved by God with His seal, His evidence, and His witness upon you. The gifts and the power manifesting through you will bear the witness of God.

> *Men of Israel, hear these words: Jesus of Nazareth, a man attested by God to you by miracles, wonders, and signs which God did through Him in your midst, as you yourselves also know* (Acts 2:22).

Jesus Himself often traced His power to do great things to His commission from the Father, and He did it in such a way as to show that He was closely united to Him (see John 5:19,30). Peter says that God did these works by Jesus Christ to show that Jesus was truly sent by Him and that, therefore, He had the seal and signs of God's approval. Jesus Himself said, "The works which the Father hath given me to finish, the same works that I do, bear witness of me, that the Father hath sent me" (John 5:36 KJV). The evidence of favor will be on everything you touch. The rod will produce. It will bring forth.

> *And with great power the apostles gave witness to the resurrection of the Lord Jesus: and great grace was upon them all. Neither was there any among them that lacked* (Acts 4:33,34a).

THE PLACE OF GIVING WITNESS

Many Christians have lacked the favor of God. Favor does away with lack! Those with the rod will not lack. Great power brought great favor and favor brought provision because of great grace upon the apostles. They had great grace because there was a great witness. They gave witness with great power to the resurrection of the Lord Jesus. Because of favor, the apostles didn't have to preach about the resurrection or proclaim it for they gave witness to it, proof, a demonstration of their divine authority to heal the sick and cast out demons.

This is where the Church is headed, to that place of giving witness—a demonstration, manifestation, proof, evidence, and testimony of personal experience and victory. God is going to prove and back up your calling. He's going to place the rod in your hand, and you will have the right and the authority to use it. Before, you had the power, but you didn't have the "right." You will now have influence, a platform, and doors will open that you never dreamed possible. You are called just as the disciples were, but Jesus selected 12 to send out with authority over sickness and demons (see Matt. 10:1). Will God select you? Has God told you to "Go therefore?"

Choose to prepare your life to receive the increase of favor. Prepare yourself to go before the King. Wait for the favor of God on your calling, on your dreams, and on your visions. Anticipate the golden scepter, the invitation to advance.

A POWERFUL WITNESS

Moses waited years in the desert for the day of manifestation. He had the promise. He had friendship. He had favor. Even though his call existed before the foundation of the world, just as ours does, it wasn't time for commissioning until God gave him the rod, the right, and the privilege to advance. The rod represented influence, authority, and divine backup—witness from God that He sent you, a witness that no man can deny.

I DECREE FOR YOU

Many are called but few are chosen (see Matt. 22:14). There is a calling. God is choosing. He's going to bestow an impartation of authority and favor. You will have the "right" to use *dunamis* power. Things will accelerate. Doors will open. The blessings of the Lord will multiply. Your destiny, visions, and dreams will birth. The latter rain and former rain will converge for harvest. I call forth the seed and the promise that's already there. Let the dew of Heaven fall upon you. Favor is coming. With the impartation of authority, chains and shackles will fall off. You will break free of tethers. The anointing will break the yoke. You will make decrees that set the captives free and proclaim liberty for those who are oppressed. God will give you what you desire. You will plunder the Egyptians and experience spiritual breakthrough. You will have the spirit of an overcomer, a victorious, triumphant spirit. The tide will change and release the spirit of the overcomer. God will fill up the holes of lack, for the blessings of the Lord will make you rich.

The rod of the one whom God chooses blossoms. As our ways please Him, He will increase His favor, measure by measure. This is the season of the manifestation of His favor.

Will you wear the crown of manifestation?

Will you advance into the tent of witness?

Position yourself for the dew of the Lord—the anointing of favor. Pursue intimate friendship with the Lord. Let yours be the rod that blooms, and then expect an open Heaven over your life as His glory comes down and manifests His supernatural, astonishing blessings on your life. Let the almonds come forth!

DIVINE INHERITANCE

INHERITANCES IN THE SPIRIT REALM

We often think of an inheritance as something physical, such as a family heirloom, a sum of money, or a piece of real estate that passes from one generation to the next when the benefactor dies. There are spiritual inheritances, however, as well as material ones. We know that there is an inheritance in Christ because believers are joint heirs, and we have been blessed with every spiritual blessing in the heavenly places in Christ (see Rom. 8:17; Eph. 1:3). Nevertheless, there are other inheritances, many in fact, that exist and are available to us in the spirit realm.

Listen. God is speaking today about divine inheritances, and He wants to release them to us. Specifically, the Lord has told me that today we are going to receive, as a Church, a revelation about divine inheritances and that we will learn how to steward what God gives us for our children's children. This revelation came to me step-by-step as I pondered various Scriptures and in particular Psalm 139:16: "Your eyes saw my substance, being yet unformed. And in Your book they all were written, the days fashioned for me, when as yet there were none of them." God has ordained destiny for every human being before birth. He has a plan, a purpose, a future, and a hope for each of us. He has good works for us to accomplish.

With this in mind, I began to seek the Lord, and I asked Him many questions, such as, "So what happens when children die and never receive their inheritance? What happens to the inheritance that You ordained for them? What about an aborted baby? What happens to that child's inheritance? What happens to the inheritances of the great evangelists of our time who die in their prime? Did anyone ever receive their mantles or their spiritual inheritances? What about the people that never reach the fullness of what You ordained for them or who never came to know Jesus Christ as their personal Lord and Savior? Did You have a future and a hope for them? Does their inheritance become available in the spirit realm? What happens in the spirit when people don't receive their inheritance? What happens to their inheritance in Heaven?"

FIELD OF DREAMS

In time, God would answer all of my questions, as I soon found out, for several years ago the Father revealed His heart to me about restoration of lost inheritances (heritages) through an amazing encounter and vision that transformed my life that I call *Field of Dreams.*

My team and I were visiting another country for ministry, and as I prepared my heart for the service, I asked of the Lord, "What do You want me to preach on tonight?" At that precise moment, I suddenly thought back to a movie I'd seen called *The Field of*

Dreams, and I saw in the spirit the slogan, "If you build it, they will come." Immediately I was in a field of dreams in Heaven, walking with the Father, but as a young boy of about four or five years old. He held my two fingers in His hands as we walked. I could only see Him from the shoulders down because He was so tall, or perhaps I was so small.

As my Father and I traveled through the field, I noticed the landscape dotted and littered with deserted military equipment and weaponry from past wars, spanning thousands of years and right up to modern-day aircraft and the like. There were WWII-like artillery shells and bombed out tanks, broken spears and shields in sand, and chariot parts, helmets, and armor.

We continued our walk in the field of dreams throughout the sands of time as though walking throughout history. The Father gently picked up and dusted off different pieces, and each time He'd heave a great sigh as though there was an ache in His heart. As He cradled each thing that He picked up, I heard Him say words like "Precious...." Then He handed pieces to me and I asked, "What are these, Lord?"

"They are lost, discarded, and broken dreams. Do you remember how David had it in his heart to build a house for Me? (God chose David's son Solomon to build the temple. See Second Samuel 7:13-14.) How many people have had something planted in their heart from Me throughout the generations but they never went and accomplished it?"

We continued our walk, and as we passed by the debris in the sand, I started to receive revelation about each piece. They all represented unfulfilled dreams, both God-given and peoples' own dreams.

"My servants," God explained, "were creative and had the dreams in their hearts but never realized them, they never came to pass. The dreams were great when they were younger, but they forgot about them…but I didn't!"

I continued listening to Him. "This is the place where dreams lay, dreams of those who did not receive Christ and never had the opportunity to walk in the dreams and visions that I had for them. Here also are dreams that never happened through great people of God who died before they saw the realization of them."

I realized that some of the dreams lay in that field as though they were in a graveyard of dreams. But then the Father said, "Todd, I want to give these dreams to you. I need someone to walk with Me in the field of dreams who will claim these promises and dream, not another man's dreams, but My dream."

I sensed the Father referred to those dreams He had not only for individuals, but also for cities and nations to claim. He wanted us to claim these promises and start dreaming God's dreams.

Over the months, the Lord taught me much more. He said and asked, "Their inheritances are available to you. Do you want them?"

I jumped on it: "Well, what ones can I have? What are the inheritances like?"

He explained that the inheritances were diverse. To one for instance, He'd planned the building of schools and universities, to another the salvation of thousands on a particular continent, to someone else an international deliverance ministry, and so on. "You can have those things, Todd, because their destinies are still available in the spirit realm."

Friends, as soon as I learned that, I went into collecting divine inheritances. What God meant by divine inheritances was the acquisition of someone else's testimony, where their story becomes your story and where what they saw God do through their life becomes reality to you. We can collect the testimonies of the works of the Lord that He's done in the lives of men and women who have lived over the past 2,000 years.

Now that the Lord had given me this revelation, I ventured further and asked Him about mantles. "Can I inherit a mantle too, Lord?"

Here's an excerpt of His response: "Todd, you don't need somebody else's mantle! You have your own."

Short and sweet, wasn't it? So the Lord intimated that while we can receive many divine inheritances, we're usually only in the right position to receive one mantle, although sometimes He will give a person more than one, as I'll explain further later in this chapter.

MANTLES

When we receive a mantle, we're receiving from God an authority, a power, a gift, and a call. Scripture tell us that Elisha the prophet had a "double portion" of the spirit of Elijah, which is, in fact, Elijah's mantle (see 2 Kings 2:9-14). As far as we know, Elisha didn't have many mantles, but we do know that he received one double portion of the mantle of Elijah. Thus, although it's rare to receive more than one mantle, God can give us a double portion of one.

So how does one get a mantle? Ask! Ask God for one. Do you know that in parts of Asia it is customary not only to desire gifts but also to ask for them? If you see something you like or want, the custom is to ask for it. We see this happen often in the Bible, like when Solomon asked for wisdom. We also know how often David cried out and positioned Himself before the Lord to know Him better, and God poured Himself into this man after His own heart. However, when we ask for something, we must also give.

Elisha asked, gave of himself in serving Elijah, and received a double portion of Elijah's mantle:

> And it came to pass, when the Lord was about to take up Elijah into Heaven by a whirlwind, that Elijah went with Elisha from Gilgal. Then Elijah said to Elisha, "Stay here, please, for the Lord has sent me on to Bethel." But Elisha said, "As the Lord lives, and as your soul lives, I will not leave you!" So they went down to Bethel. Now the sons of the prophets who were at Bethel came out to Elisha, and said to him, "Do you know that the Lord will take away your master from over you today?" And he said, "Yes, I know; keep silent!" Then Elijah said to him, "Elisha, stay here, please, for the Lord has sent me on to Jericho." But he said, "As the Lord lives, and as your soul lives, I will not leave you!" So they came to Jericho. Now the sons of the prophets who were at Jericho came to Elisha and said to him, "Do you know that the Lord will take away your master from over you today?" So he answered, "Yes, I know; keep silent!" Then Elijah said to him, "Stay here, please, for the Lord has sent me on to the Jordan." But he said, "As the Lord lives, and as your soul lives, I

will not leave you!" So the two of them went on. And fifty men of the sons of the prophets went and stood facing them at a distance, while the two of them stood by the Jordan. Now Elijah took his mantle, rolled it up, and struck the water; and it was divided this way and that, so that the two of them crossed over on dry ground. And so it was, when they had crossed over, that Elijah said to Elisha, "Ask! What may I do for you, before I am taken away from you? Elisha said, "Please let a double portion of your spirit be upon me." So he said, "You have asked a hard thing. Nevertheless, if you see me when I am taken from you, it shall be so for you; but if not, it shall not be so." Then it happened, as they continued on and talked, that suddenly a chariot of fire appeared with horses of fire, and separated the two of them; and Elijah went up by a whirlwind into Heaven. And Elisha saw it, and he cried out, "My father, my father, the chariot of Israel and its horsemen!" So he saw him no more. And he took hold of his own clothes and tore them into two pieces. He also took up the mantle of Elijah that had fallen from him, and went back and stood by the bank of the Jordan. Then he took the mantle of Elijah that had fallen from him, and struck the water, and said, "Where is the Lord God of Elijah?" And when he also had struck the water, it was divided this way and that; and Elisha crossed over (2 Kings 2:1-14).

Now in those days, although the mantle was a cloak (the Hebrew is *addereth*) it was metaphorical and significant of the anointing that was upon Elijah. A mantle typically was a large garment worn over the clothes and probably made of sheepskin, but according to some theologians, it appears this was Elijah's only garment and probably fastened by a strip of leather,[1] so he depended upon that cloak as his daily covering.

As a side note, the Bible also applies the connotation of a mantle (the Hebrew is *me'il*) to the "robe of the ephod," a blue tunic woven without a seam that reached below the knees and was put on by being drawn over the head. This was worn by priests, kings, prophets, and rich men. It was the "little coat" which Samuel's mother brought to him, year after year, in Shiloh, a miniature version of the official priestly robe.[2]

Getting back to our Scripture text above from Second Kings, we see that Elisha *asked* for a double portion of Elijah's spirit, and it is noted that Elijah replied it was a "hard thing." It's not always easy to get the mantle of another, much less a double portion, but the key is to ask.

WHERE TO FIND A MANTLE

Elijah told Elisha that he could have the mantle *if* Elisha saw him as he passed into Heaven. That meant Elisha had to be there with Elijah all of the time so he wouldn't miss the opportunity. If Elisha really wanted it, he'd have to do everything in his power to get it, even if it meant becoming, in effect, closer than his mentor's shadow. Elisha persevered and stuck like glue to Elijah and received the double portion because he wouldn't leave his side. The principle of note is that if you want to receive a mantle from God, stick to Him like crazy glue. Earnestly desire His highest will and His highest plan for your life.

When Elijah died, Elisha tore off all of his clothes and wore the mantle as Elijah had as a full and sole garment that had just as much significance and importance to him as it had to Elijah.

While Elisha lay on his death-bed in his own house (see 2 Kings 13:14-19), Joash went in to mourn over Elisha's impending death, uttering the same words that Elisha spoke when Elijah was taken away, "My father, my father! The chariot of Israel, and the horsemen thereof."

The very corpse of Elisha resuscitated a dead man. After his death a dead man's body was laid on his grave, and as soon as it touched his remains, the man revived and stood up (see 2 Kings 13:20-21). In life, and even in death, that mantle wrought great wonders! It happened because he touched the double portion of the spirit of Elijah, residing upon Elisha's bones.

It's interesting to note that when Elisha died, no one asked for his mantle. I'd like you to keep this in mind as I recount a vision a young man shared with me many years ago. His vision had great effect on me, and to this day, it's always at the forefront of my mind because of its great significance as far as our potential destinies are concerned.

In his vision, he arrived in a valley where he saw mantles resembling the garment of Elijah that Elisha wore. He saw mantles lying on the ground that belonged to Smith Wigglesworth, Kathryn Kuhlman, Martin Luther, Moses, Abraham, and others—mantles that had been upon the lives of great men and women used of God throughout history. He saw mantles as far as his eyes could see. Some of the mantles looked new as though never worn, others barely used, and some quite worn and tattered.

These mantles are indicative of the availability of many mantles today. We too may outgrow a mantle, and it too would lay available for someone else to wear. We can ask for a mantle as Elisha did (Elijah *invited* Elisha to ask) and the Lord God will give it if it's His will (see 2 Kings 2:9). However, when we ask, we may not have a specific one in mind; therefore, God will offer us one of His choosing. I believe His offer comes when He sees our passionate desire for Him above all else, including the mantle.

I mentioned earlier that God usually gives us one mantle, but there are instances where, when we are faithful and grow into one (or outgrow another), God will drape us with a new one. The first mantle the Lord placed upon my life was an evangelist's mantle. I put it on and remained faithful with it and eventually grew into it. Two years later, God offered me a new mantle and said, "Do you like this one?"

I liked it but didn't quite understand what it was and asked, "What is it, Lord?"

He explained that it was a prophet's mantle. I tried it on, but it didn't fit quite right. Of course—I was comfortable in my old mantle; this would take getting used to. Sometimes when we wear a new mantle, it doesn't seem as though it fits, but we can grow into it just as I did. We may feel awkward at first or on display, but God always chooses wisely. People may notice at first and say, "Hey, wow, look what's shown up on your life, buddy!"

I had to get comfortable with the prophet mantle and now it fits really well, like a glove. God came along again though and offered me yet another one. "Todd, I have a new mantle for you, look at this one!" It was the mantle of an apostle. As soon as I saw it, I said, "God, I don't want that one. I'll wear my evangelist's mantle and the prophet's mantle, but please don't put that apostle jacket on me. It doesn't look right or feel right and besides, I'm just getting used the prophet's mantle."

It didn't take me long to surrender to the Lord and receive the apostolic mantle. I'm still growing into it. We grow into these things. The mantles will grow up with you. Do you remember when God brought the children of Israel out of Egypt? They were 40 years in the wilderness, and they wore the same clothes and the same shoes for those 40 years. As they grew up, their clothes and shoes grew with them. As such, we grow into our mantles and our mantles also grow with us.

In all, God gave me three mantles, although not the mantles of any great person of old—at least I don't believe so—but they may be available, and don't be surprised if you find yourself cloaked anew or afresh from time-to-time.

INHERITING THE DESOLATE INHERITANCES

What did our forefathers leave us as an inheritance? On the surface it may look like not much because for the most part we don't remember the great revivals of the past, say, 200 years ago. However, many ministries have ended and leaders have died without passing the spiritual baton over to another. Consider some of the great evangelists of the past whose sons or daughters haven't carried on the work of the Lord or the mandate He gave a mother or a father. Some never inherited the work of ministry or carried it through to the next generation. However, I believe the Lord is about to restore and release these misplaced, lost, or forgotten anointings upon certain believers. In describing the glory of the Messiah's ministry, the Lord said through the prophet:

> *In an acceptable time I have heard You, and in the day of salvation I have helped You; I will preserve You and give You as a covenant to the people, to restore the earth, to cause them to inherit the desolate heritages* (Isaiah 49:8).

Have you ever thought about inheriting the desolate heritages of others? *Heritage* means "inheritance, legacy, and birthright." God said to me, "Todd, I will cause men and women to receive desolate heritages!"

The Holy Spirit then brought forth from Isaiah:

> *Those from among you shall build the old waste places; you shall raise up the foundations of many generations; and you shall be called the Repairer of the Breach, the Restorer of Streets to Dwell In* (Isaiah 58:12).

How exciting—the foundations of many generations! Is there a generation today that God will entrust with the foundations of generations long past and since lost? Can we rebuild those foundations for God? Is it actually possible to come into the very inheritance of the generations of long ago and possess its fruit today? I believe it with all of my heart, with a resounding "Yes!" Think about the potential in the raising up of the foundations of *many* generations.

As Repairers of the Breech and Restorers of Streets to Dwell In, there will be those anointed for restoration, that is, those whom God will appoint to help restore the paths of many destinies, for there are many crying out to God today asking for the prophetic answers to "Where am I? What is my purpose? What's my future; where do You want me? I'm in the wilderness and things seem so far away!"

Isaiah also prophesied about the good news of salvation and the anointing to preach the good news, to heal, to proclaim liberty to the captive, and to loose the bound (see Isa. 61:1). Jesus was the fulfillment of this prophecy (see Luke 4:17-20). However, read on in Isaiah 61 and see what God also says:

> *And they shall rebuild the old ruins, they shall raise up the former desolations, and they shall repair the ruined cities, the desolations of many generations* (Isaiah 61:4).

That's quite the addendum. Here we see God saying, "I'm looking for history-makers—men and women today to whom and with whom I can entrust the former, desolate heritages to repair."

God's heart prompted me to say, "I'll step up to the plate God; choose me! I want those inheritances," because I realized that our accomplishments today can only be as great as the shoulders that we stand on. Our momentum in the spirit carries on from the momentum of our forefathers. The Kingdom of God advances—we start where they left off, and we move forward, and as such, the blessings compound.

Compound blessings—what an exciting thought. Nevertheless, as I've emphasized before, this is not to say that we just inherit and that it doesn't cost us something—it's always going to cost us!

GENERATIONAL BLESSING AND INHERITANCE

What do you want to leave to your children and their children's children? How about a dynamite spiritual momentum and mature spiritual stature, whereby they get to start at as a high a level and as quick a momentum as you can possibly leave them? The spiritual sons and daughters that have passed through my ministry and anointing today will begin their respective ministries at the level it took me seven years to learn how to build. That's where they all start. They will never start small with 10 or 20 people, but they will have the potential to preach to entire crusades full of lost or ailing souls. There are evangelists out there right now who have passed through our ministry doors with itineraries booked in advance for a year because of the association they had with my ministry and anointing. They came under my influence (not unlike how Elisha came under Elijah's influence) and thus were positioned to receive the inheritance of my previous years of ministry.

They don't have to start from the bottom, up. If it's God's will and choosing, they can leap right into the momentum and level that I was at when I discipled them. It's sad though today that many spiritual parents don't want to nurture their children this way—whether they feel threatened by it, or for whatever reason. We must think differently. I'm thrilled when I see how, when God chooses a man or a woman to mentor under me, He thrusts them to even greater levels than me. Jesus Himself said that we would do great and greater works than we saw Him do, and I trust that these people will do great and greater works than me. This is something we should all strive for in bringing up natural and spiritual children. It's how Christ taught, because He was determined that we would advance the Kingdom, and that means constant movement and infilling of the Kingdom of Heaven in the world.

God thinks from the beginning to the end and about everything in between all at the same time. Thus because the Kingdom advances, looks forward in terms of the generations that are to come, He's already thinking about our grandchildren and great-grandchildren to come. Why don't we? We're always in the now mindset; but I tell you, why not work toward a great inheritance for them? Imagine the spiritual blessings you can leave them. Imagine the foundation you can build for them to work from. Listen, when God gives you a prophetic promise, do you ever think past how it will come to fruition in your own life? Do you look past that and think about the foundation of that vision that you can lay for your children? Can you think about it in terms of making those dreams, visions, and prophetic words concerning your destiny available also to your offspring and their offspring, natural and spiritual?

Sure, it's exciting when God promises us something—we're like children who want to spend it right away. "Look what my Daddy gave me, and guess what He's promised?" How about building that promise up to such a degree that those blessings will literally be like fountains and deep wells for your children to draw from?

It's sad, but the majority of our young people inherit mostly religion and tradition; but what if instead we all stored up and left rich spiritual heritages to our children? If you don't inherit the Promised Land, they may. Why not give them a head start? Their floors can begin on our ceilings!

CONSIDER GOD'S TIMING

"He remembers His covenant forever, the word which He commanded, for a thousand generations" (Ps. 105:8). When God gives a word, He thinks about the word in the context of a thousand generations. However, when we receive a word from the Lord, we're so excited about it happening "right now." And understandably so because every gift from the Father is bound to be exciting. Trust though that if you don't see something happen in your lifetime, it doesn't mean the promise or word is dead. That word is good forever and can apply to a thousand generations. Why not think about laying that foundation, of course with the thought of seeing it, but also with the assurance that if you don't, your children or their children or their children's children will? As such, you may stand to inherit a word or promise given to someone of long ago—perhaps a word He gave to King David, to your great-great-grandfather Olaf, or even to someone now who has fallen away from Him.

There are many churches out there today that haven't lived out a prophetic word or promise they've received, for various reasons, perhaps because the leader died, or attendance died, or the church had to be torn down to make way for a highway. Whatever the reason, the word isn't lost! Another church can step right into that promise. Maybe your church has stepped into a promise from a little white church on a prairie somewhere 200 hundred years ago. Perhaps your ministry is picking up where another ministry failed.

God's word never returns void, He will always fill it and fulfill it (see Isa. 55:11). He's given His word to thousands upon thousands, but even though those people are dead now and long forgotten, His word is still alive and active. You might be on the Internet one day, scouring the archives of the sayings and ministries of people of long ago. You'll realize that something the Lord promised that ministry or person hasn't materialized, so you can say, "God, even though that promise is 400 years old, I want it Lord! I want to resurrect that and claim it as my inheritance!"

Listen, if I should die before my time, I would expect someone to step up and gather all of the dreams and promises God has given me for my ministry and advance every one. And before that person dies, he or she can tend that plant or seed and plant it into future generations, and so on. The nature of the Kingdom advances, pursues, overtakes, and recovers all (that's the title of our next chapter).

In Generational Terms...

His counsel stands forever, the plans of His heart to all generations (see Ps. 33:11). That's the nature of God. When God spoke to Abraham, He *saw* Isaac. When God spoke to Isaac, He *saw* Jacob, and when He spoke to Jacob, He *saw* Joseph. When God saw Joseph, He *saw* you and me, because all the families of the earth are blessed through Abraham. When God spoke to Abraham, it wasn't just a word to Abraham, but for all generations, and so on. Get the picture? We can inherit the same dreams and visions that God promised to Abraham: "And I will bless those who bless you, and I will curse him who curses you; and in you all the families of the earth shall be blessed" (Gen. 12:3).

Here was God saying, "I want to bless the generations to come in the exact same way that I bless you, Abraham." What an awesome blessing when you think in terms of it being a blessing for a thousand generations. Weighty, heavy, rich, sweet.

Psalm 78 paints a beautiful picture of the generational mindset of God. Here is an excerpt:

> *For He established a testimony in Jacob, and appointed a law in Israel, which He commanded our fathers, that they should make them known to their children; that the generation to come might know them, the children who would be born, that they may arise and declare them to their children, that they may set their hope in God, and not forget the works of God* (Psalm 78:5-7a).

At my present age, I'm thinking about my life, ministry, and what I'm building, but even though I'm not of grandparental age, I'm already thinking about my children's children and what kind of inheritance I can leave them. I also think about what I leave to my mentorees, or spiritual children, for I have a responsibility to these upcoming generations. When God moves, He moves throughout the generations, so today is the set time to research and discover lost heritages and to ask God for them. Many of us are sitting on spiritual goldmines and we don't even know it. These spiritual goldmines will advance and fill the earth with the glory of God. We can also set about creating new legacies, not just starting from where another left off, but also trusting that, whichever way God leads you, from this day forward everything will affect future generations.

Now what happens after the "thousand generations"? Do the inheritances just drop off or are we cut off from them? David answers this beautifully, "The Lord knows the days of the upright, and their inheritance shall be forever" (Ps. 37:18). Perhaps he was remembering God's promise to Abraham and his descendants—that theirs' was an everlasting covenant and inheritance (see Gen. 17:7). So how about it? Can you change your way of thinking to include generations in the context of eternity as it relates to God's plan for your life?

PROPHETIC DOWNLOAD

The Lord prophetically downloaded revelation to me concerning our divine inheritances:

I saw angels like wind, fire, and light going out of the Church like a flash of lightning, and God illuminated the Book of Hebrews: "And of the angels He says: 'Who makes His angels spirits and His ministers a flame of fire'" (Heb. 1:7).

As I saw these angels going out with great speed into different regions of the world, the Holy Spirit spoke to me through another Scripture in Hebrews: "Are they not all ministering spirits sent forth to minister for those who will inherit salvation?" (Heb. 1:14).

Salvation is an inheritance. The Holy Spirit spoke to me that there are angels that are released right now like light: "The entrance of Your words gives light; it gives understanding to the simple" (Ps. 119:130). I saw the angels going forth with the inheritance of salvation on behalf of family members who need to receive salvation.

They will inherit salvation. That's a prophetic decree! God is saying that our inheritance will be souls, for this inheritance God gives to people, ministries, and churches. Imagine inheriting more than a few new souls a week…how about 1,000? It is harvest time, and thus I speak forth this decree into the heavens: "I declare a whole new evangelistic anointing over the Church. From this day forward, we'll grow by souls!"

GO FORTH INTO YOUR INHERITANCE

So, have you decided what you want to inherit? Perhaps you already have. You'll know. What do you do when you know you've inherited a heritage? Go forth, for this is the set time for the advancement of God's Kingdom, and it's about to advance in an unparalleled manner because of the compounding of the momentum since the beginning of time. Prophecies from the past few decades are happening now.

A few years ago, the Holy Spirit impressed upon me some prophetic words given in Kansas City in the 1980s for the Generation X set. At the time, the word of the Lord was about a "Joel's army" that would arise—a nameless, faceless generation who would do great exploits for God. They would be a spiritual army of young and old who will not fight with human weapons but with militant love and the raw power of God! Many prophets have spoken about this huge revival army of millions of radical soldiers whom God is training to aggressively take ground for the Kingdom of God under the authority of Jesus Christ.

Stadiums would fill with seekers and mighty miracles, and this would be the start of a great harvest. I vocalized my thoughts aloud and said to myself, "Generation X is older now, they've aged, so therefore we're either completely off, we've miscued the word of the Lord, or we're sitting on our backsides just waiting for God to do it all!"

The Lord answered my wonderings and said, "Todd, aren't those prophecies awesome?"

"Those were awesome God!"

"They were about a particular generation. You know that word—it hasn't come to pass yet. Even though the generation is older, the prophetic word still stands true."

I suddenly realized that the problem was that everyone waited for the vision to come to pass, instead of stepping into it.

"Would you like to inherit those prophecies, Todd?"

Would I! Could I? "Yes, I'd love to have them!"

"Well," God directed, "Go rent a stadium." And I did. Hallelujah! Later, Fresh Fire Ministries became involved with the building up of a Joel's Army training center.

Do you know what I became? A first fruit. Some of those prophets have declared the fact, because although many heard and received those prophecies of the 1980s, most did nothing with them. It's one thing to receive, but another to step into. I knew God's very clear promise to me previously—that I could become a forerunner concerning prophetic words if I claimed them as mine, even though I didn't live in Kansas City or know of the prophets and prophecies at the time. It didn't matter; I claimed them in my heart anyhow. Those were the words of the Lord, unchanging for generations, alive, active, real, and powerful, and I knew I fit the prophecy and claimed it.

FOLLOW THROUGH

Don't claim it if you don't plan to walk it. Don't receive it if you don't plan to claim it. Don't ask for it if you don't plan to receive, claim, and walk in it. Apply action to prophetic dreams, words, and visions, and act like now is the time. How much further into the future are you waiting for? Don't forget, another can fulfill anything you leave undone, but you build that foundation, and you can leave the top of the tower as their floor for starting.

I've learned that when God gives me a prophetic word and I take it fully into my heart, it's a "go!" No question. The moment I receive a word over my life, to me it is permission to go forth. How many heritages of the past were lost because people waited? How many seeds never were planted, never were watered, never pruned? God wants to redeem inheritances in this generation.

LEGAL RIGHTS

We can begin inheriting God's promises today. Before one of my meetings, the Holy Spirit told me that there would be someone there upon whom I was prophetically to "give," on the Lord's behalf, the inheritance of revivalist Aimee Semple McPherson. I said, "God, how is that possible?" He explained that the person He would point out to me had a generational tie to Aimee in her family tree and thus had legal right to it. I gave and spoke the word over the person, and she confirmed the details God had given me concerning her.

I don't know what it was about Miss McPherson, but another time while I spoke about inheritances and about her, a man jumped up and said, "Todd, you're not going to believe this! The Lord told me to bring to the meeting with me the Bible that Aimee Semple McPherson had signed for my grandfather on the day he was ordained as an associate minister to her ministry." Therefore, this man had the legal right to claim the inheritance of his grandfather, simply because of his connection to this great woman of God. The inheritance, therefore, can be in the physical family lineage and transmitted through the generations (see Num. 27:8-11; 36:6-8).

There may be great preachers in your family line that you didn't even know existed. Know though that what they labored for, you have legal right to and you can build from where they left off. Yes, you can even inherit their influence and favor as a direct descendant. Examine some of the great evangelists of our day, like Billy Graham and his son, William Franklin Graham III. He, by all appearances, seems to have inherited his father's mantle, and he has built on the foundation that his father has laid. He's also taken incredible ground through the organization he founded known as Operation Christmas Child, a huge global mercy project started in 1993 that invites families to fill shoeboxes with presents for distribution abroad to the poor. The organization reached 7.3 million children in 2005 alone with the love of Christ, impacting those lives for eternity.[3]

While he may have the legal right in the natural to his father's ministry, he has legal right in the spirit according to God's will for his life, and his offspring also have that legal spiritual right.

It may well be worth the time to delve into your family tree, just to check out potential legal inheritances in the Lord. You may find that you're a first generation Christian, but don't let it surprise you if you find believers down your generation line.

It could be that you don't find any people in your lineage to draw from as an inheritance source, but that doesn't mean you have no inheritances because you have many brothers and sisters in Christ Jesus too, as well as spiritual fathers and mothers whose heritages are all available to you in the Spirit.

Often their inheritances die with them because so few people realize the truth about divine inheritance; thus there aren't that many searching.

What's To Inherit?

When God gives you a divine familial inheritance, He gives you the same dream and the same word that He gave your benefactor. Even if you've never before received a prophetic word over your life, you can collect because those dreams, words, and visions still exist in Heaven. Go ahead, claim one, and then act on it, just as I acted on the prophetic word for Kansas and sought to fulfill it by the establishment of a Joel's Army training center. Others can prophesy it, and you can claim it as your own; however, you will want to be faithful with it, so it's imperative that you spend time in the presence of the Lord for strategy in using it.

1. Inherit Mantles

God also wants you to know about inheriting mantles. Recall my earlier story about the young man's vision of the valley strewn with mantles. In that same vision, the Lord told him to pick a mantle, whatever he chose. What a dilemma, for he had many to choose from! He saw the mantle of Elijah, Elisha, Abraham, Jacob, and others, and it was as hard to pick one as it would be for a child to pick just one piece of candy from a candy shop. Just when he thought he was in a pickle, a shiny mantle caught his eye. It didn't look like the other ones at all, but in his spirit, he sensed that no one wanted this one, that it was one often overlooked or dismissed.

Who did this mantle belong to? Enoch! He chose it right away.

Perhaps no one wanted it because the Bible says that one day "Enoch was no more," and most people don't want to be here one day and gone the next (see Gen. 5:24 NIV). What they overlooked is that Enoch walked with God...*walked* with the Creator of the Universe! All this young man wanted was to walk with God as Enoch had, and He passed God's test in rightfully choosing for that stage of his life. Because this youth's choice so pleased the Lord, the Lord released an "unlimited invitation" to choose another mantle, almost like giving him *carte blanche* or handing him a platinum card with an unlimited Kingdom limit on it. Praise the Lord! Imagine the mantles he could ask for. Imagine if Solomon's mantle were available. Wow.

2. Inherit the Kingdom of God

Yes, all believers in Jesus Christ will *enter* the Kingdom and will *see* the Kingdom of God, but there's also an *inheritance* of the

Kingdom of God which doesn't necessarily happen to every believer on earth.

The writer of Hebrews says, "...that you do not become sluggish, but imitate those who through faith and patience inherit the promises" (Heb. 6:12). Those who press in by faith and have patience will inherit the promises. We don't have to give in to discouragement, because we can encourage ourselves in the Lord all the time, as David did (see 1 Sam. 30:6 KJV).

3. Inherit Blessings

> *Finally, all of you be of one mind, having compassion for one another; love as brothers, be tenderhearted, be courteous; not returning evil for evil or reviling for reviling, but on the contrary blessing, knowing that you were called to this, that you may inherit a blessing* (1 Peter 3:8-9).

Here we see an example of positioning ourselves to inherit a blessing. In this instance, we love one another, not only because we're members of the same Body of Christ, not only for the sake of those for whom Jesus died, but we also love one another for our own sake; by blessing those who have done us wrong, we shall inherit a blessing. If you cannot love someone for Jesus' sake or for the sake of those whom He loves, then love for your own sake, because blessings are the fruit of it.[4]

4. Inherit the Glory

"The wise shall inherit glory, but shame shall be the legacy of fools" (Prov. 3:35). It's not the glory of this world or honor among men that we inherit, but an eternal glory with Christ Jesus that we receive as a gift at the bequest of the Father, which comes to us as His children through the death of Christ.

SIX INHERITANCES IN THE BLESSING OF ABRAHAM

1. A Great Nation

When God spoke to Abraham, He "saw" each one of us, because in Abraham all the families of the earth are blessed. We covered this a little earlier in the chapter where I noted that God told Abraham that He would bless those who bless him and curse those who curse him.

God wants to make our families, our ministries, and our churches great nations, that we would enjoy their fruitfulness and success. He wants to make nations out of our loins. We may only ever birth one dream, but that dream can touch a nation. He may give us many dreams, we may adopt the dreams of others long before us, He may set us upon foundations already built, or He may move us into a speedy momentum of advancement for the Kingdom.

2. A Great Name

You have a right to these blessings that God has for you in the spirit realm. He wants to make your name great, to favor you, and to exalt you with a good name and a good reputation—a name that will precede you—a name generations will remember because God made your name great (see Prov. 22:1). How badly do you want a great name for His glory? God is into your name! A good name is better than "precious ointment" (see Eccles. 7:1).

Just the name of the nation of Israel brought dread to their enemies because God made their name great (see Gen. 35:5). A great name is vital for a believer.

3. *Financial Prosperity*

God wants you to give out of abundance and not lack. How can you bless others financially if you don't have anything to give? It's OK to think of blessings from a material standpoint when Kingdom endeavors and advancement are at stake. God also doesn't want us living in poverty—we are to be examples to the world of His abundance, His grace, His generosity, His creativity, His wisdom, and His favor. Imagine a world of financially wealthy Christians who consistently and always give all the glory to God while at the same time understanding that their wealth all belongs to Him. Imagine how we could use His financial blessings in our witnessing efforts. God wants to bless you; you are a child of a King of unlimited wealth.

We can come into a financially prosperous inheritance through the Lord's provision. The servant tells Laban about God's generosity to Abraham, his master, on whose behalf he has come for the master's son, Isaac, as they seek a bride: "The Lord has blessed my master greatly, and he has become great; and He has given him flocks and herds, silver and gold, male and female servants, and camels and donkeys" (Gen. 24:35).

Before I went into ministry, I was financially poor. Poverty followed several generations before me. I tried to find jobs, and then I'd be laid off and end up on welfare or financial assistance of some kind. I just could never seem to get ahead. However, as I became faithful with a little here and a little there, God brought increase to me and to my ministry, and I've tried to be a good and faithful steward of all He has entrusted to me.

It's so exciting to know that we have inheritances that will be passed to our families and generations thereafter. "Houses and riches are an inheritance from fathers," and this includes spiritual fathers as well (Prov. 19:14). As a spiritual father to many in and through this ministry, I want to declare that every ministry associate, intern, son, and daughter that we raise up in Joel's Army, in our ministry schools, and in our conference seminars and crusades, and everyone that has ever been a part of the nation that God has given me in the spirit, will never lack any good thing that God has for each one. I decree that every single one has a right to my spiritual inheritance because of association. Just as God blessed Abraham, so am I blessed and so are you in the mighty name of Jesus.

Sometimes it's hard to relate to Abraham because he lived so many thousands of years ago, but if you don't believe the prosperity gospel, I urge you to go back and study the blessings of Abraham and the amazing inheritance God promised him. It's in the Word; it's for us, too. Don't be misguided, don't misinterpret what the Word of God says is ours today, don't confuse the truth with your own preconceptions. God desires financial prosperity for His children. Abraham was rich in God, and God made him rich. God promised to bless him—anything less is profoundly not God's fullness for our lives.

4. Victory

God wants to give us victory over our enemies: "And blessed be

God Most High, who has delivered your enemies into your hand" (Gen. 14:20). The moment we claim the inheritance of Abraham, we will be overcomers, and our enemies will be delivered into our hand because of our association with Abraham. We are victorious by association

5. The Manifest Presence of God

God promises us His presence. He promised Abraham His presence. Here God speaks to Isaac of the promises He made to his father: "Dwell in this land, and I will be with you and bless you; for to you and your descendants I give all these lands, and I will perform the oath which I swore to Abraham your father" (Gen. 26:3). Again, God confirms His presence right down that family line, this time with Jacob: "Behold [I love that] I am with you and will keep you wherever you go" (Gen. 28:15). Do you know what that is? That's divine protection in the presence of God Most High. Place your name in that Scripture verse and recite it aloud. "Behold, I am with you, Todd, and will keep you wherever you go." Now say, "Behold, God is with me, He will keep me wherever I go!" Amen!

6. Restoration of Unfulfilled Heritages

We've covered much on this subject, but it's fitting to place it here at the end of the chapter because victory, exaltation, and favor are God's will for us today, and He will bring restoration and renewal to everything that we've lost. What have we lost? Testimonies, inheritances, dreams, visions, abundance, victory, and favor, and there's no doubt more that the enemy has stolen or that we've let go of. They are strewn about the field of dreams, waiting for you to reclaim and fulfill with the Father's help.

I believe God wants to take some of you reading today into that place in the spirit to show you what the inheritances are. The psalmist said that, for those who delight themselves in the Lord, God will grant to them the desires of their heart (see Ps. 37:4). You know what you have to do to claim them as your own. Seek God first above all else, pursue Him with all of your might, and then let Him take you into His field of dreams and mantles to choose the one you want. Be faithful with it, act on it. And know that the Father delights as you clothe yourself every day in His precious mantle and go in search of desolate treasures that will advance the Kingdom for His ultimate glory. Become part of a company of believers anointed to bring restoration of lost heritages to others so that they, too, would be restored upon destiny's path for the filling of the earth with His glory and presence.

KINGDOM APPLICATION

- Think about your life's ministry and the type of legacy you can leave for generations to come.

- Uncover what God has already promised, or start a new legacy.

- Seek the plans and counsel of the Lord (see Ps. 33:11).

- Go and do it, now.

- Ask God for a mantle; surrender and receive it.

- Collect every word, vision, and dream spoken into
your life. Search for ones that you want. Claim them,
step out, and fulfill them.

⟶ PERSONAL PRAYER

Father, thank You so much for the wine and honey of Your Spirit. Oh Lord, I want to dream. I want to dream big! I want to partner with You in my dreams. I want to walk, no, run with You in Your field of dreams and forever change the way I think and see. I want to run through it, Lord, with laughter, joy, hope, and expectation coursing through my heart and the refreshing breeze of the Holy Spirit lifting me high for glorifying You. I want to experience and fulfill my dreams, Your dreams, our dreams for the harvest. Jesus, where there is capping and quenching in the Spirit, release me into the fullness of dreaming big with You. Incubate my dreams in the Spirit, and plant in my heart the desire, the vision. Oh I hope for, and expect, and long for a big dream. As I lay on my bed and meditate on and draw from my heart those dreams and visions that I never thought possible in the natural, I call them forth from Heaven, right now. I birth and call forth those things. Forgive me for failing to act on the words and prophecies I've received in the past. I claim them now, and search for ancient words of long ago, never fulfilled. Please release that realm of the Spirit. Release the honey and the wine so that I can drink of Your Spirit—even as

I sleep tonight—and birth every treasure which is Your calling. I ask these things for Your glory, Father. In Jesus' name. Amen.

━━◦ CORPORATE PRAYER

Father, I want to thank You for releasing upon me the anointing to bring restoration that will cause men and women of God to come into their inheritances that have been lost for many generations. God, by the prophetic word I release over men and women today, I release desolate heritages. I decree that this generation will be the one that will raise up the foundations of many generations, and what has been lost in the past will be manifested and will come forth today. It will show up in our lives, in our churches, in our ministries, and in our nations. Thank You, God, for these inheritances and that Your blessing— the blessing of Abraham—is coming upon us.

God, take those men and women who are ready into the field of dreams and release the anointing that will cause every dream and every vision that You desire to be restored. Please show us what the inheritances are and where they are. We want to receive the desolation of many generations. God, Your Word remains for a thousand generations, and we will take that dream, and we will take that vision, and we will take those inheritances.

We want to discover our families' divine inheritances, and we want to claim those inheritances for our lives and our children's children's lives. God, we claim our families' inheritances. We claim the godly divine inheritances of prior generations in our families. Father, please bring us revelation in this matter so that we have understanding as to what the inheritances are.

We have come to realize that we can acquire the testimonies and inheritances of great men and women of faith. We want to come into inheritances like this Father. We don't want to miss one single inheritance that You want us to have. We want to inherit the same inheritance that You gave to Abraham. You made his name great, You made him a great nation, You made him a great blessing, and You delivered his enemies into his hands. Father, Your presence was with him, and you gave him material blessings so that he could be a blessing to others.

We are also aware that You planned great healing ministries to bring glory to Your name, but many never happened. Also, there are men and women You called into a powerful worship ministry, but they never had a chance to walk in this anointing. There are those whom You destined to build Your Church and to walk in a deliverance ministry, but this did not occur. We want to receive those lost inheritances, Lord. We'll take healing inheritances, deliverance inheritances, prophetic inheritances, inheritances of church-planting, mission work, and all the resources that You promised men and women. We'll take these inheritances today, Lord, in the name of Jesus.

God, we claim the inheritances, the dreams, and the

visions for our cities and our nations. Those visions that You gave the great revivalists in our nations, we claim them. We thank You for bringing us revelation about divine inheritance. We step into the dreams, the visions, the prophetic promises, and the inheritances. We realize it's the set time, and we say that they are coming into our lives, in the name of Jesus. We will watch for them. We will build up what has been ruined, and we will repair and raise up the former desolate heritages from past generations, in Jesus' name. Amen.

ENDNOTES

1. Matthew George Easton, *Easton's Bible Dictionary* (1897), s.v. "Mantle," http://www.studylight.org/dic/ebd/view.cgi ?number=T2408 (accessed 27 June 2008).

2. Ibid.

3. *Operation Christmas Child*, www.operationchristmaschild .org (accessed 20 November 2007).

4. David Guzik, "Commentary on Hebrews 6," *David Guzik's Commentaries on the Bible* (Enduring Word Media, 1997-2003), http://www.studylight.org/com/guz/view.cgi ?book=heb&chapter =006 (accessed 27 June 2008).

PURSUE, OVERTAKE, RECOVER ALL

There's just so much that God is saying, and yet He has given me a specific word, a prophetic declaration, precisely for this hour. This is not just a word *from* the Lord, but is a word *of* the Lord. What I am about to share is something that God is saying to the Church today, and He wants you to contend for its manifestation.

The word of the Lord is actually three commands in one: *pursue, overtake, and recover all.* These are God's weighty words spoken to David before he became king during one of the most volatile periods of his life, caught in the midst of a grueling *spiritual* battle fraught with nasty warfare in the *natural* (see 1 Sam. 30:8).

Listen! Because of where God wants to take us in terms of advancing the purposes of Heaven on earth in the midst of the battle-plan of the enemy to oppose it, we absolutely have to understand how to activate, integrate, and employ these commands into our lives today. Many believers are ready; how about you? Are you ready? If you have a good foundation of intimacy in the secret place, of regularly practicing the presence of God, then this is vital as it under-girds several more prophetic revelations that I'll share with you here. However, if you don't have that intimacy with God, I urge you to spend a lot of quiet time with Him before and while you embark on this part of your spiritual Kingdom journey.

GOD'S WEAPON OF CHOICE: PRAISE AND WORSHIP

We are coming into a new season where worship will have its place as a vital and powerful weapon against warfare. God is anointing the high praises of His people and releasing victory in warfare in the midst of it. Worship, in fact, is God's weapon of choice as we answer the call to war in the heavenlies. God is pouring out a fresh worship anointing upon believers today whereby men and women of God will have faces as lions. This is scriptural. Let's lay a firm foundation for this prophetic revelation by glimpsing the life of David as he prevailed against the enemy when the Amalekites raided his camp (see 1 Sam. 30:1-2).

David and his army were men of renown and so feared that when David was set to go to war against Saul (allying with the king of Gath and the Philistines), the Philistines would not allow him to take part in the coming battle because they weren't quite sure where David's loyalty stood (see 1 Sam. 29:1-11). Perhaps they speculated that he would turn in the heat of battle to win back Saul's favor. Thus, David and his men were forced to pull out of the war, and they returned to Ziklag, the place given back to them as a gift by the king of Gath (see 1 Sam. 27:6). Ziklag was a significant stronghold for David, and it is an important prophetic symbol for us as a place with an anointing and a call. Located in the southern part of Judah, the place was an inheritance of Judah (see Josh. 15:1,31). Ziklag actually *belonged* to the children of Judah, and this is significant because the word *Judah* means "praise."

This was their inherited city where they lived and kept their possessions, but perhaps even more importantly, it was a place where the mighty men of valor arrived daily to help David "until there was a great army, like the army of God" (1 Chron. 12:22b).

The Bible likened David's army to the army of God! David wasn't even king yet, but he had enthroned himself in the hearts of these valiant men who trusted him to lead them. They were a mighty army and assembled in the city of praise, so no wonder it was as God's army. The prophetic significance of the city to us today is that Ziklag really was an apostolic training center and mission base that trained young men's hands for war.

ATTACK ON PRAISE

Forced to return home to his stronghold of Ziklag from the war zone, David and his crew arrived to a devastating scene. While he and his men were at war, the Amalekites raided the city. They kidnapped all of their loved ones and burned the camp to the ground. When David and his men saw the disaster, they were so grieved that it exhausted them. They deeply mourned the loss of their loved ones and David, once the men's hero, soon lost his credibility. They even spoke of stoning him to death, and naturally this distressed David. They had been forerunners of the day, on the cutting edge, seeing breakthrough and victory. These were mighty men, leaders, the next generation, a Joel's army, and yet they wanted to stone David whom they had once trusted.

What would you do in such a shaking? How would you react if you saw your home burned to the ground and your family gone, held captive by the enemy? Let's put it into a more personal perspective. You return to the loss and there's nothing but ashes, for the loss is everything you are. Everything is gone—your family, your friends, your business, your finances, your vision, the anointing upon your life, God's call, your ministry—everything is ash and in a heap. That's a dark night of the soul, and David and his men were in it.

Ziklag, an inheritance of Judah, a symbol of praise out of which triumph should come, now lay in a heap of ash. Hear me. The Lord told me: "Todd, this happens to the Church when it forgets the power in praise, because praise brings triumph. Where there is no praise, the city is burned with fire."

The enemy attacked praise in attacking the city of praise. He's attacking praise in this hour—your praise, our praise. The good news is that the Lord won't let the enemy's plans triumph over us.

BECOME A WORSHIP WARRIOR

The Lord told me that those who took up the weapon of praise would have the greatest victory, that real praise would determine our victories. This doesn't mean a little worship here and there, worship only when we go to church or in the car on the drive to the store. This means full-on warrior worship, using the sword of the Lord in your hands and the high praises of God in your mouth "to execute vengeance on the nations and punishment on all the peoples; to bind their kings with chains, and their nobles with fetters of iron; to execute on them the written judgment" (Ps. 149:7-9).

This is a tremendous anointing and promise for those who take up these high weapons. In the darkest of hours, the sword of the Lord in your hand will do its work by the high praises of God in your mouth. This is a God-breathed truth, and it will bring great deliverances to you. Triumph will be supernatural. At the "sound of an earthquake," instantly your loved ones will be set free. The prison doors will open and their shackles will fall off just as the chains that fettered the apostles Paul and Silas fell off as they released high praises behind the prison bars (Acts 16:25-26). At the sound of high praise, the Word of the Lord will go forth as a sword for victory in your warfare. The Lord is anointing the high praises of His people that will release triumph!

YOU NEED TRUE GRIT

In David's great distress over the enemy's raid, coupled with the threats of death from his own men, the Bible says, "David strengthened himself in the Lord his God" (1 Sam. 30:6). David's inner determination to strengthen himself in his God worked with God's determination to strengthen him in return. Something awesome was released to David when he worshiped God and purposed to press in to the Lord's heart in his time of tribulation. Think about that, because David's inner resolve lights the way for us today. It shines through like a powerful truth that we can grab a hold of. We must resolve and determine to press into God in the heat of the battle just as David did.

David's true grit shines as a major key to becoming a warrior worshiper. Becoming one is crucial to overcoming any weapon formed against us. David's critical choice to strengthen himself in his God actually inspired him to carry out a vital act that caused him to catch God's eye. This act released the counsel of God to David for war. God's counsel was to pursue, "for you shall surely overtake them and without fail recover all" (1 Sam. 30:8).

It is so important that in the heat of intense spiritual battle we press in to God's heart if we are to make sound decisions that will release His favor and counsel. You have to know what to do when all of hell breaks out against you.

TAKE RADICAL RISKS

God has often tested me in healing ministry. One time He said, "Todd, let's see if you will really pray for another thousand if no one in the first thousand is healed." Man, I had to press through many times when the deaf didn't hear. But I had God's word that it would happen, so I went the distance! We have to stop tiptoeing around Heaven and get real revelation of God as truly the rewarder of those who diligently seek Him (see Heb. 11:6).

It's easy when you're in church, taking a healing school, or in a healing meeting of some kind to believe God for things. What about when you're not there—when you're home, right in the midst of battles? What are you going to do when you pray for your son or daughter who is addicted to drugs? Will you pray and then stop if he or she isn't delivered or you see no results? Do you know that some pastors won't even go to the hospital to pray for the sick just in case God doesn't heal? They pray for the comfort of God over the person—but they are afraid of defeat. We can't be timid anymore. We can't leave a back door open to rush out of so that we can save face if nothing happens. We have to persist. I can't tell you how often I've said, "OK now, I'm going to war, and I will contend. I won't give up." So, when is enough enough? Ask yourself, "Am I dead yet?" If you pinch yourself and you find yourself still around, then keep praying, keep warring, keep believing, and keep contending. Keep on asking, keep on seeking!

You're in a war, we all are, and this is the hour to inquire of the Lord and stand firm in His counsel. Our stealth depends on this so that we can daily break through and triumph. The enemy is in contention over God's destiny in your life, and you are in battle, even if you're unaware of it now.

We saw how the enemy attacked the prophetic city that was a training ground for emerging leaders—essentially a supernatural training center of sorts, where warriors were the interns who were taught, imparted to, and then released for battle.

STRENGTHEN YOURSELF IN THE LORD

I respect and identify with David. Talk about a hero of faith. Just as he was about to be stoned to death by the men he loved, he pulled aside to seek his God. With the stench of acrid smoke still in their nostrils, grief-stricken over the loss of their families, they determined to kill the one who'd led them so faithfully.

The very destiny of David's city of Ziklag was at stake, as was his personal destiny. There he stood at his ordained divine threshold, about to be murdered. What he chose to do marked his future, and he chose well. He set himself apart with his God in the secret place for strength. Shut in with God, David's inner determination to strengthen himself in his God and to believe God's prophetic promises worked together with God's grit to strengthen him in return. David indeed received all of the true grit he needed to stand firm as Israel's great leader while remaining spiritually sensitive to carry out a very important act.

SEEK GOD'S WISDOM AND COUNSEL

What did he do? What was his action that carried the day? Scripture says that David spoke to Abiathar the priest. He said, "Please bring the ephod here to me" (1 Sam. 30:7). David identified with this holy, priestly garment because it symbolized the true intentions of his heart, which was his deep love and respect for God. He also knew from experience that the ephod represented God's counsel and *advice* (see 1 Sam. 23:9-12). Wisely, he asked for the ephod. He took off his armor and, with great reverence, the man after God's own heart put on the priestly garment. That's when God gave him the directives to pursue, overtake, and recover all, and David could do that because he had the strength of the Lord, the assurance of the Lord, and the presence of the Lord.

We are in desperate times that require desperate measures, and desperate measures require God's wise counsel and His strength to pull us through. We have to catch God's eye and inquire of Him,

"Shall I pursue this troop? Shall I overtake them?" We must position ourselves to hear His counsel.

Many believers right now are standing at a personal divine threshold. You may be contending for the salvation of your family and loved ones, for the anointing, for faith, for vision, for ministry, even for your city, but whatever it is, God is declaring to you today to pursue, overtake, and *without fail* you will overcome and recover all that the enemy has stolen. If, as David did, you enter into the secret place of God's presence as a worship warrior, He will strengthen you for battle. When you inquire of Him, your God *will* release to you His heavenly counsel. In the darkest night of your soul, you can count on God to show you what to do next. I know this to be true, because the Lord has done this for me.

For more than a year, I was in the process of the "dealings of God" in my life. For a while it felt as though all of my passion had gone—my passion for God—which of course caused me to lose sight of my vision, my ministry goals, and everything I loved. Everything seemed lost.

One day it was all there, and the next I heard the Lord say, "Dark night of the soul." Almost instantly, everything I loved about serving the Lord was gone, and I couldn't do anything about it because it was of the Lord God's will. When God puts us on the rock and it feels as though we're going through a crusher and being grinded into powder, it doesn't feel good.

All we can do in that hour of the dark night is to determine within ourselves to strengthen and encourage ourselves in the Lord. If we don't, discouragement will defeat us. We must remember what God promised us. Listen. If we are going to be ready for what I believe God is releasing today, we have to strengthen ourselves. To do that we need a little shot of joy and oil, and wine and glory. That shot comes by taking to heart four main keys:

1. *Desire God above everything else:* As the psalmist, all of our desire will be for God; our soul will pant and thirst for the living God (see Ps. 42:1).

2. *Remembering God's faithfulness:* Remember His supernatural breakthroughs, deliverances, salvations, healings, and prophetic words to you (see Ps. 63; 1 Tim. 1:18-19).

3. *Build yourself up in your most holy faith:* Pray in the Holy Spirit, not forgetting the hidden power of praying in tongues (see Jude 1:20).

4. *Face the giants:* Face the giants that tried to take you out in the past (see Jude 20:1-48).

When you receive and apply these keys to your life, you will be almost or nearly ready to go to war and plunder the enemy's camp, but before you go, God wants to complete your preparation by pouring out a new fresh anointing on you.

A FACE LIKE A LION

In this anointing, the Lord wants to terrorize the enemy by

giving you a face like a lion. One division of David's army, the Gadites, was from the tribe of Gad. The division was comprised of 11 "mighty men of valor, men trained for battle, who could handle shield and spear, *whose faces were like the faces of lions,* and were as swift as gazelles on the mountains" (1 Chron. 12:8). They were the fiercest tribe in all of Israel. Little wonder, because each one had the face of a lion! *That's* an anointing!

Scripture details each of the division's members by providing us with each of their names; the meanings of the names give us great insight into what it takes to become a fierce warrior. Note that there were two Jeremiah's, thus the following ten names. Read on, because this is fascinating.[1]

1. *Ezer/Ezar*: Treasure

2. *Obadiah*: Servant

3. *Eliab*: God (of his) Father

4. *Mishmannah*: Fatness

5. *Jeremiah*: Appointed by God

6. *Attai*: Timely Fit

7. *Eliel*: Strength, Mighty

8. *Johanan*: Merciful

9. *Elzabad*: God has bestowed

10. *Machbannai*: Native of the Land (Machannite)

Here were the fiercest and most ferocious men in the land, and yet they were men of all of those attributes. They were a help and a treasure, men of mercy with servant hearts. They were the wildest men, but they knew the Father's love and His appointed time. They were the most aggressive, and yet they knew how to trust the Lord and that God would provide for them. Yes, they had faces like lions, for they were those whom God called into His mighty army.

God wants to anoint your face like a lion's face with a fierce spirit that comprises the qualities we see in the division of Gad. Cry out to the Lord for this anointing because it will empower you with a godly vengeance to pursue, overtake, and recover everything the enemy tears down, puts asunder, burns, steals, and ravishes.

PARTICIPATE

Pursue literally means to advance or gain ground on something. This involves an action on your part. Equally, the word means to continue to annoy, afflict, or trouble,[2] to endeavor to overtake, to go in pursuit of, to chase, to pursue, to prosecute.[3] The battle won't be easy, but God will give you the holy persistence that will empower resolve in your heart not to give up.

Overtake means to come upon unexpectedly, to take by surprise,[4] to move ahead of, to catch up. When we overtake something we're taking it by surprise by catching up and passing it.[5] Do you regret decisions you've made? Did they set you back? God is saying that this is the time to catch up, redeem the time, and overtake.

Recover means to get back or regain (something lost or taken away), to make up for or make good. *Regain* suggests success in recovering something that has been taken.[6]

As soon as David received God's command to attack the Amalekites, he proceeded immediately to pursue and hunt down his enemies (see 1 Sam. 30:8-16). Finding them spread across the land celebrating because of their great spoil, David and his mighty army swiftly attacked and overtook them. It was a long battle that lasted from twilight until the evening of the next day. Rather than paraphrase this text though, I want you to read it for yourself, because it describes a victory mightier than I can ever describe:

> *Then David attacked them from twilight until the evening of the next day. Not a man of them escaped, except four hundred young men who rode on camels and fled. So David recovered all that the Amalekites had carried away, and David rescued his two wives. And nothing of theirs was lacking, either small or great, sons or daughters, spoil or anything which they had taken from them; David recovered all. Then David took all the flocks and herds they had driven before those other livestock, and said, "This is David's spoil"* (1 Samuel 30:17-20).

David recovered all. Can you imagine what that would mean in your own life? There are things you don't even know you've lost, but

God promises total recovery. What have you lost? Your health, your peace of mind, your stature, your favor, your finances, your family? This is the hour to pursue the enemy, to overtake him, and to recover all, and I declare and stand firm with God that victory is your promise.

Listen, somebody has to break through and get the fullness of God's Kingdom back into the Body of Christ! We can't be afraid of failure. We have to be ready to go instead of wondering why God is sending us. People often wonder why God pulled me out of the pit of drugs and alcohol. Why did He take me out of the sawmill when I was nobody and say, "Todd, I want to send you all over the world with the Gospel and with saving, healing, delivering power"? When God told me that, I didn't spend time wondering why or how, I just said, "God, I am willing. Here I am—send me. I can hardly wait Lord! Even if I face opposition, persecution, or reproach, even if I have to fight in a spiritual war, praise God—that is for me! I am not going to be destroyed for a lack of knowledge; I will believe Your word. Whatever comes my way in reproach, because I choose to believe You, I know You will move in miracles."

We have to press in if we're going to pursue, overtake, recover, regain all. We can't be afraid of failure. We need courage. When we step out in faith to lay hands on someone for healing, for instance, we have to believe that God will honor our action. We must persist!

By faith we shall overcome even the roaring lion that goes about seeking whom he may devour (see 1 Pet. 5:8). God can easily subdue all who set themselves against Him.

Don't slacken the pace. Lay hold of the promises of God. We have to "see" areas of death coming to life, promises resurrected, and dreams fulfilled.

⟶ Kingdom Application

Lift your hands, praise Him, and seek His strength and counsel. Encourage yourself in the Lord and you will be mighty in battle. God is searching for those with the heart of David and the attributes of the division of Gad. Spend time in the secret place, take up the ephod, and remain strong in the Lord.

God is releasing sweet companionship, for He desires friendship and fellowship with you. At the same time, He's releasing that fierce spirit upon men and women so that they will be persistent in battle, never giving up, shutting up, or letting up until they recover all.

When I got saved, I needed the enduement of "power from on high" (see Luke 24:49). I needed the Holy Spirit to empower me to fulfill my destiny. I vividly remember my first Holy Spirit power encounter. I was in my home praying, "Lord, I want to know what it is like to have Your power come on my flesh," and I prayed this often. As I lay on my bed one night crying out in this way, His power came—and it felt like a 500-pound weight pressing me into the mattress. I couldn't even lift my head off of the bed—let alone my arm! What I can only describe as a Holy Spirit current that felt like electricity, coursed through my body exploding within me. This current felt like wave after wave of electricity, and my whole body shook and vibrated with the power. I couldn't even lift a finger.

Although the Spirit of God came to fill me with His power that night, it wasn't enough to endue me with power over the next decade—I would need to keep myself full of God's power so that I could take Christ's healing touch to the world. Those fresh touches continue to come through intimacy with God. I wait on the Lord, pray in the Spirit, and contend for power until I feel my faith rise and my spirit strengthen. I invite the Holy Spirit's presence to come, and I invite His power to come on me for the impossible to happen. The disciples went forth endued with power—and I want to go forth with that same *dunamis*, dynamite, explosive, and miracle power of God. You have to be willing though to pay the price in faithfulness with your authority and time invested with God. Unleash all of the supernatural resources God has given you and fight for your destiny. Battle for your city. Contend and press in for your children and their children. Look in the mirror now. Do you see the face of a lion? Get set for the roar of the Lion of the Tribe of Judah. It's all systems go!

Lift up your voice to the Lord and praise Him. Give praise to the Lion of the Tribe of Judah, Christ Jesus. He is releasing an anointing of warfare in our high praises so that we can be like the mighty men, like the army of God, fully equipped to pursue the enemy, overtake, and recover all. This is God's will for you. Take it and unleash the fullness of your potential in Christ Jesus for the glory of the Lord and the advancement of His glorious Kingdom, in Jesus' name.

ENDNOTES

1. All names except "Jeremiah" [appointed by God] (see Jer. 1:4) taken from *Strong's Exhaustive Concordance of the Bible*, s.v.v. "Ezer/Ezar" [treasure] (Hebrew #687), "Obadiah" [servant] (Hebrew #5662, #5647), "Eliab" [God (of his) Father] (Hebrew #446), "Mishmannah" [fatness] (Hebrew #4925), "Attai" [timely fit] (Hebrew #6262, #6261), "Eliel" [strength, mighty] (Hebrew #447, #410), "Johanan" [merciful] (Hebrew #3110, #3076, #2603),

"Elzabad" [God has bestowed] (Hebrew #443), "Machbannai/ Machannite" [native of the land] (Hebrew #4344, #4343).

2. *Dictionary.com Unabridged,* vol 1.1, s.v. "Pursue."

3. *Webster's Revised Unabridged Dictionary,* s.v. "Pursue."

4. *The American Heritage® Dictionary of the English Language,* 4th ed., "Overtake."

5. *Dictionary.com Unabridged,* vol 1.1, s.v. "Overtake."

6. *The American Heritage® Dictionary of the English Language,* 4th ed., s.v.v. "Recover, Regain."

FINAL THOUGHTS

The world may call us crazy, but Jesus calls us His disciples, His friends. Amen! As His disciples and friends, we are ordinary believers filled with an extraordinary obsession with God, and if you're not thus obsessed, you should be. God's called you out of the literally dead-end road of living for yourself and into His call for you to stand out in the world, just as Christ stood out in the crowds.

You are a supernatural citizen of a supernatural Kingdom with a supernatural call on your life. You're not your own man or woman. You belong to Jesus! The King of kings and the Lord of lords! Wow! This Kingdom is rising and filling; it's constantly in motion, advancing and increasing. It's time to unleash the full supernatural *dunamis* potential that God has seeded in you for a watchful world.

Use your priestly authority to loose yourself from the fetters and demands of religion, tradition, and the legalistic mindset and into the dynamics of living an overcoming, triumphant, peculiar, and spectacular life as God created you to live it. Breathe Kingdom air. Feel the wind of the Spirit. Swim in the living water of His presence. Walk in the harvest fields with Jesus. Get out there in the battlefield. Wield your weapons. Trust in the power of the Gospel. Follow Jesus! Get ready; get set for an uprising of eternal proportions not seen since the days of the first century church, whereby the earth will shake to its very foundations in preparation for the coming of the Lord and the invasive rising of His Kingdom—and the glory of the Lord will rise in you exactly for that purpose.

I'm so excited about *Kingdom Rising*'s sequel! In it, we will raise the bar and learn how to contend, live, and battle for the supernatural standard of living that will cause a tearing down of strongholds and an uprising of heavenly proportions. It will empower you hungry ones who are willing to pass through this age to the glory of the Kingdom of God's age.

My heart is to help equip you to overcome what hinders you from operating in the mind of Christ. We'll wage war for the heart, mind, and emotions, and identify and understand the opposition and tear down strongholds. You'll learn how to experience the Kingdom, the manifestation of Kingdom glory, and contend for Kingdom encounters. We'll activate your spiritual sight for 20/20 vision and break into your responsibility to win souls for Christ. We'll pursue the reality of the Kingdom in your life and understand how to sow and reap as you go all out, trusting in the power of the Holy Spirit working in and through you.

I want you to pursue all of this knowing that it will be incredibly different from anything you've ever experienced—a supernatural order above all others.

God has chosen gladly to give you the Kingdom (see Luke 12:32). That's a promise.

Fresh Fire to You!

FRESH FIRE MINISTRIES

Fresh Fire Ministries is an international ministry called to global harvest. Todd Bentley and the FFM team take God's saving, healing, and delivering power to the nations of the world, sparking revival fires and equipping the body of Christ in power evangelism and healing ministry. FFM conducts healing crusades throughout Africa, India, South America, Mexico, Europe and beyond. Hundreds of thousands have been saved, delivered and miraculously healed. Each year, Fresh Fire also hosts several conferences, teaching schools, and anointing services, accommodating the training and equipping of thousands.

Fresh Fire is also active in humanitarian and mercy ministry, communicating the gospel of Jesus Christ, not only in word and power, but also in compassionate action. This practical ministry includes the building of orphanages and homes, feeding outreaches, providing medical supplies and treatment, and clothing distribution.

Our vision is to see people revived in a new passion for Jesus, burning with the fire of evangelism to reach the lost. We achieve this goal through conferences and training schools, the Jesus Road School Intern Program, the Supernatural Training Center seven-month equipping program, and short term missions trips to the nations.

For more information about:
Todd Bentley and Fresh Fire,
FFM missions trips, ministry partnership, and all of our
resource products, please visit our website.

Fresh Fire Ministries
P.O. Box 2525 Abbotsford, BC, Canada V2T 6R3
Phone: (604) 853-9041 Fax: (604) 853-5077 Email: info@freshfire.ca
www.freshfire.ca

How to get started In your ministry
Just pick a problem, find someone's story
That moves The heart of God & say Yes!
Don't let Anyone Define you!
Only God!